ZEN DOODLE CATS and DOGS Coloring Book:

Color Amazing Zen Doodle CATS&DOGS!

By Jane McKenty

* Based on the Best Zen Doodle Drawings of Jane McKenty

Table of Contents

Introduction

Conclusion

Introduction

This book was created based on the books "**ZEN CATS: Drawing Amazing Zen Doodle Cats**" and "**ZEN DOGS: *Drawing Zen Doodle Dogs*"** where we were explaining the drawing process of Zen Doodle with Amazing Cats and Cute Dogs.

Here you will find the final pictures which you can color with any style you want. So if you do not want to know the full process of how to draw them you can enjoy coloring them as you wish. Enjoy!

Zen art of drawing or Zen doodling really helped me a lot to penetrate into that oasis of peace that we all carry inside of us and is buried under the everyday concerns and disturbances. I meditate for many years, but not on a daily basis just because I often can't just sit doing nothing.

So, Zen doodling is a perfect blend of meditation where you are "doing something" that is creating the drawings, after which you can somehow use it. You can even paint or draw a true artistic picture without any former knowledge of drawing.

It is attractive and engaging to draw a variety of complex motifs that come from our subconscious to paper squares, popularly known as tiles. But even more fun is to fill a variety of known forms with more or less tangled Zen patterns and motifs.

In this book you will find five amazing cat drawings drawn by the art of Zen doodling and six beautiful drawings of Dogs. Kittens in this book are in their respective positions, gazing across the back, stretching or proudly and elegantly standing on their paws. Also you will find different breeds of Dogs for those who love small cute dogs and for fans of "dangerous" dogs like a Bulldog.

Here is a preview of what you'll find for coloring in this book:

<u>Cats:</u>

- Cats on the moon
- Cat's stretching

- Cat looking back
- Cat's dream
- Queen Cat

Dogs:

- Maltese
- Chihuahua
- Beagle: the Head
- Beagle: the whole figure
- Basset
- Bulldog

Enjoy!

Cats on the moon

I assume this cute motif of two kittens sitting on a crescent moon with their backs turned toward the watcher is known to most of you. This motif can often be found in amateur paintings, coffee mugs, T-shirts, notebooks and wallpapers. If you always wanted to know how to draw these two legendary kittens, the drawings below are for you.

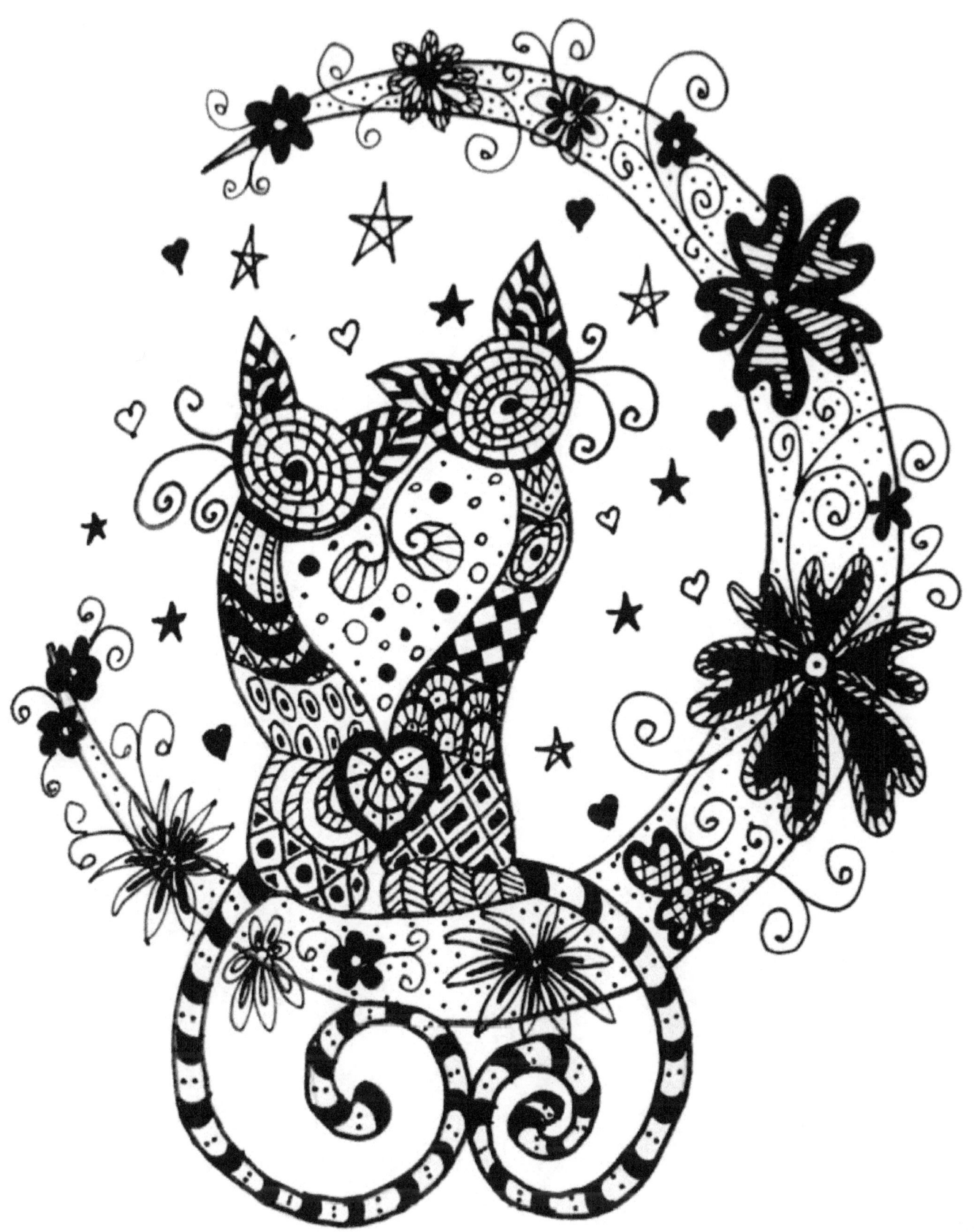

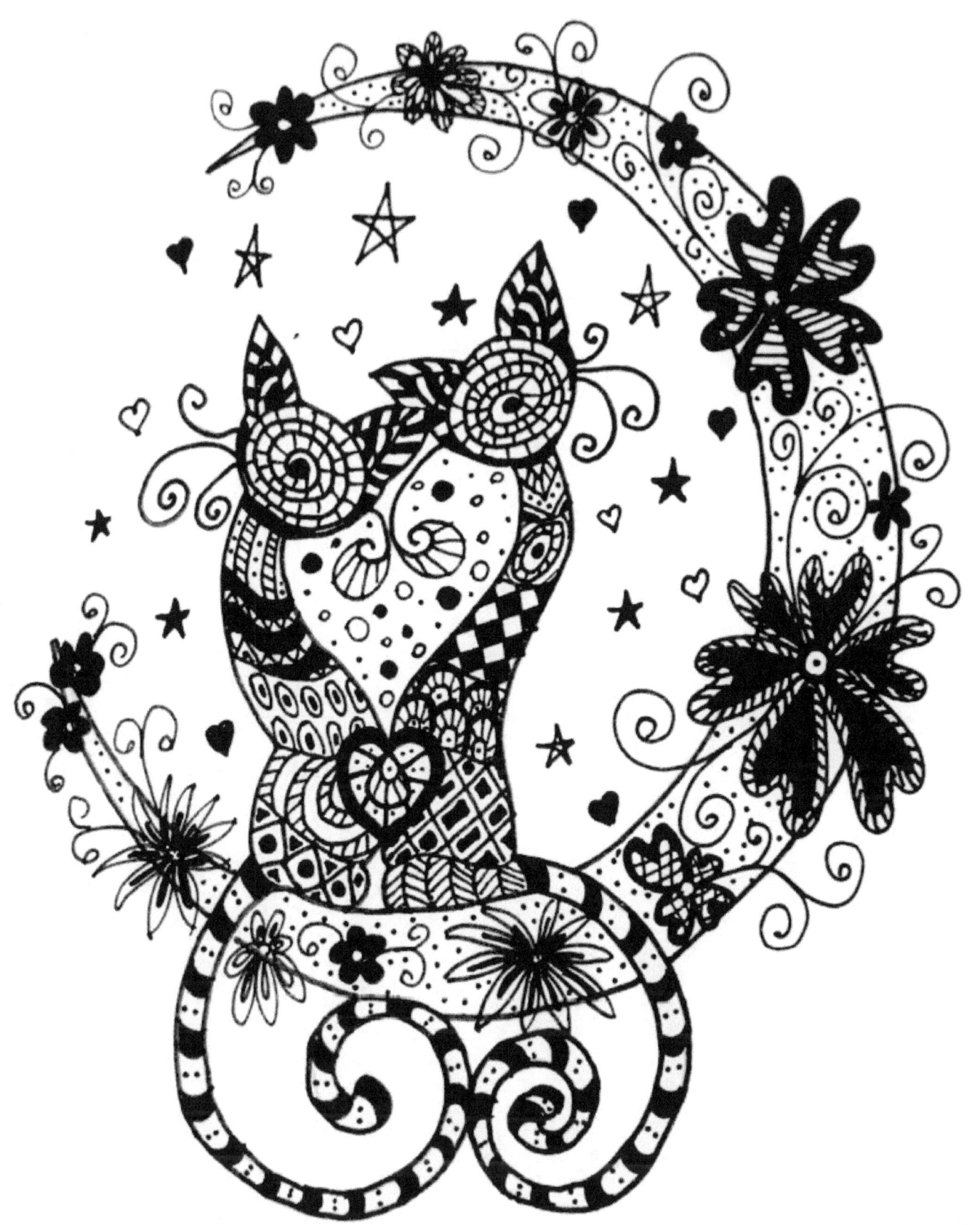

Cat's stretching

One of the most common and favorite movements of a cat is stretching after sleep. Some believe that cats are real artists in being lazy and that they can sleep up to 16 hours a day. Of course, a good sleep is always followed by a good stretching.

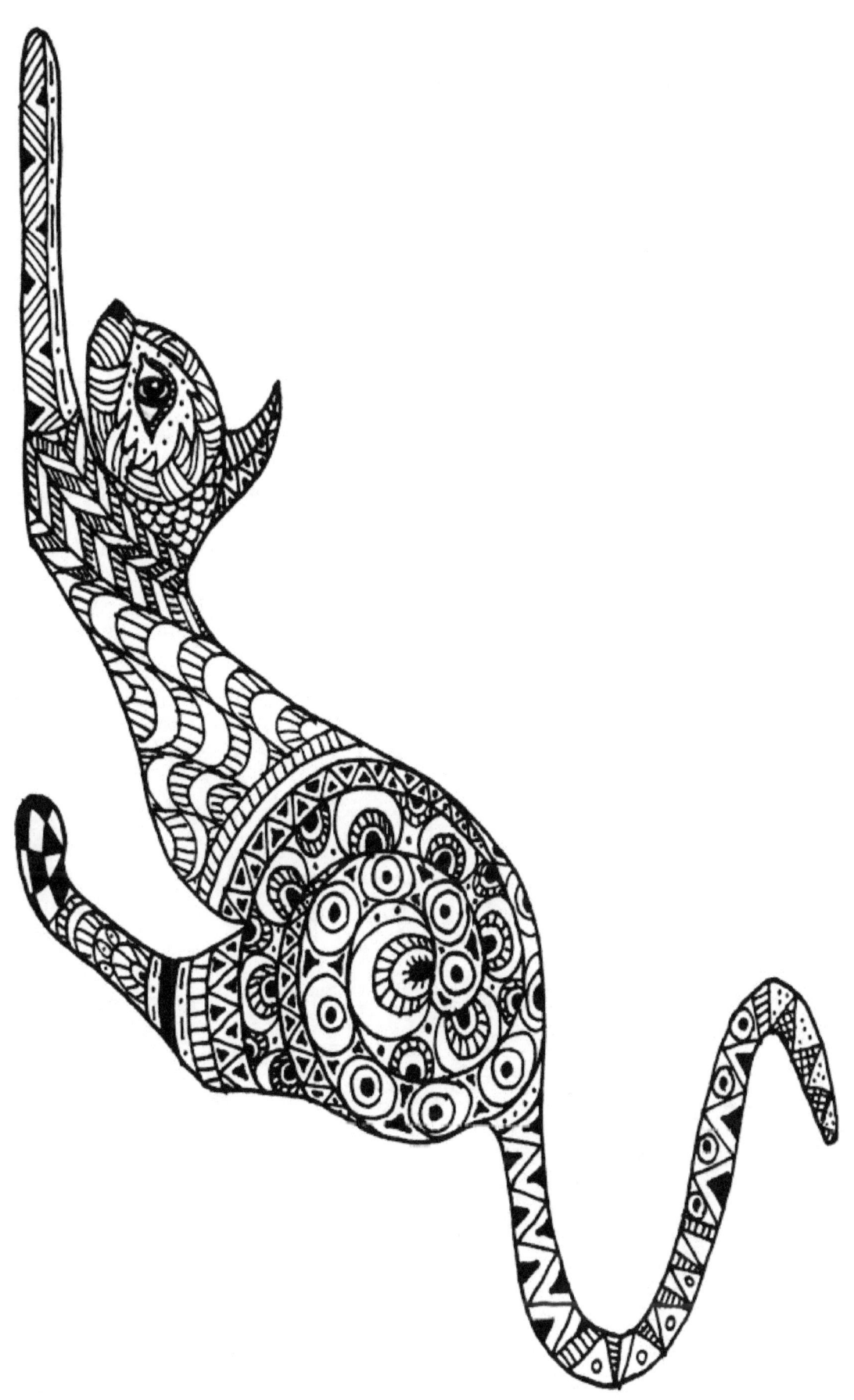

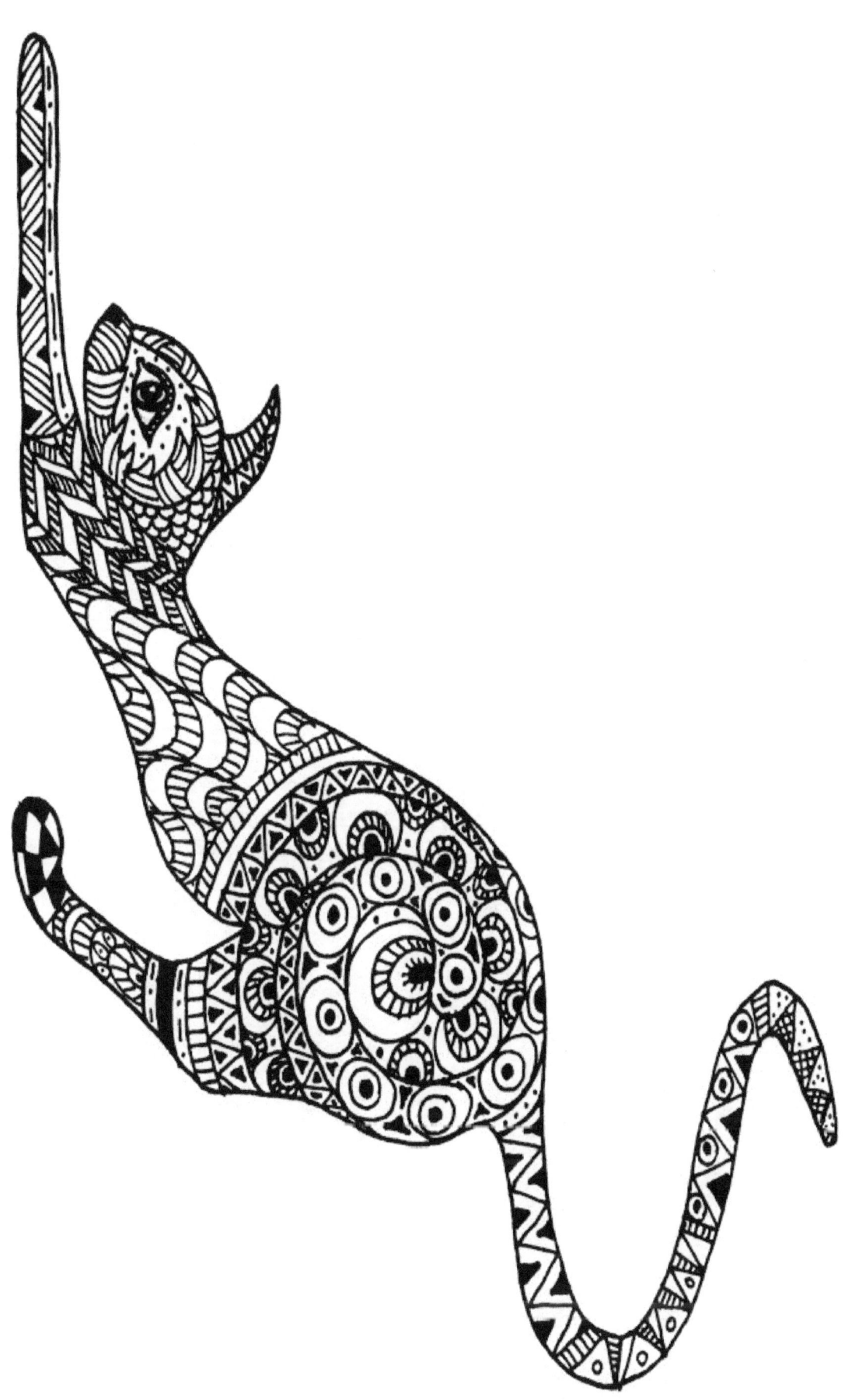

Cat looking back

The great Renaissance artist and scientist Leonardo da Vinci said that even the smallest cat is a masterpiece. The same can be said for the next drawing of the Zen cat that looks back. This pose is also very specific to cats. It seems as if they are too lazy to turn the whole body or as they pose to some famous painter.

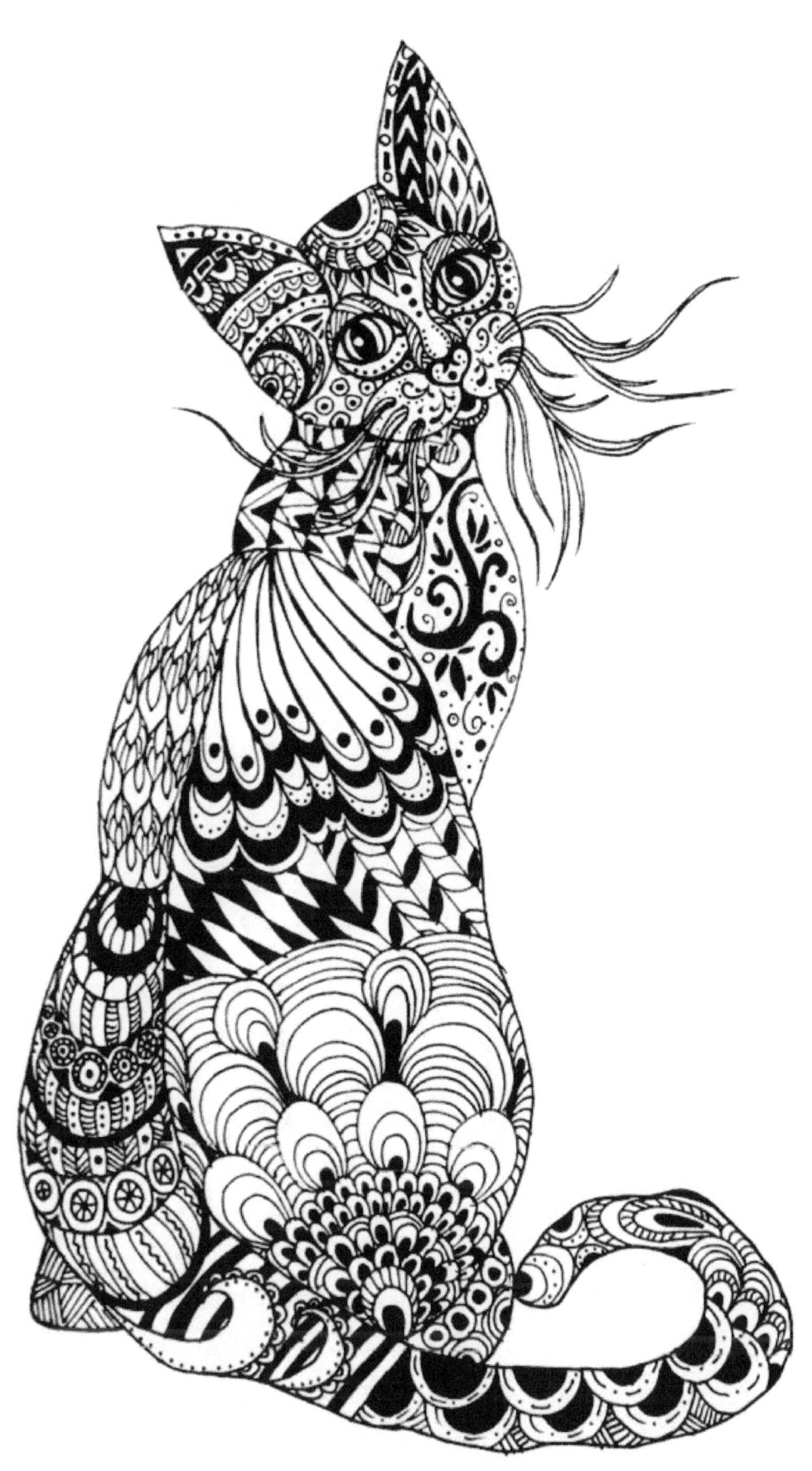

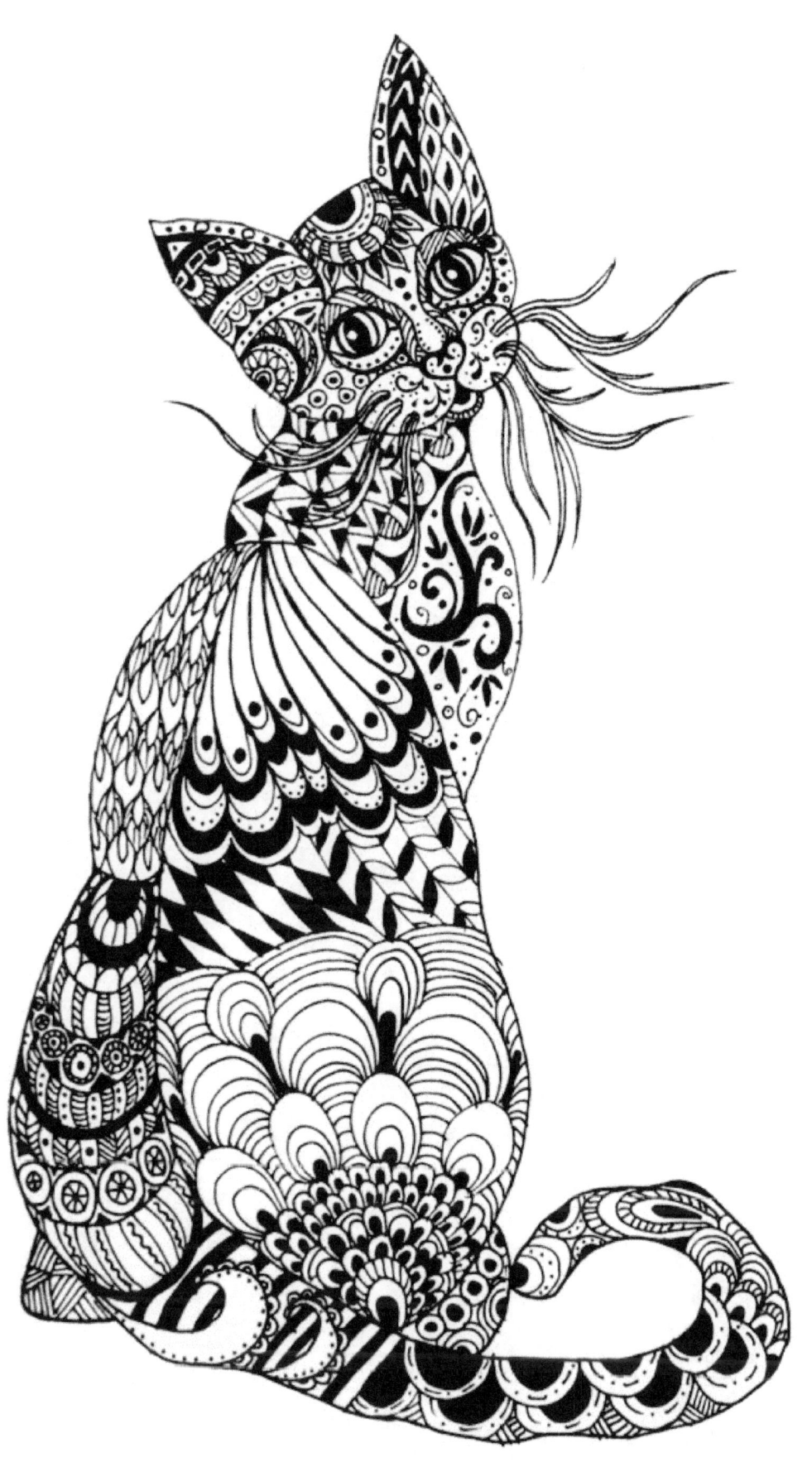

Cat's dream

What that could be: a cat's dream? A cat can only fantasize about mice or fish. In our case, the fish is in question. I present you the Zen cat captivated by daydreaming, and what she's imagining is much, much fish that the cat loves to eat.

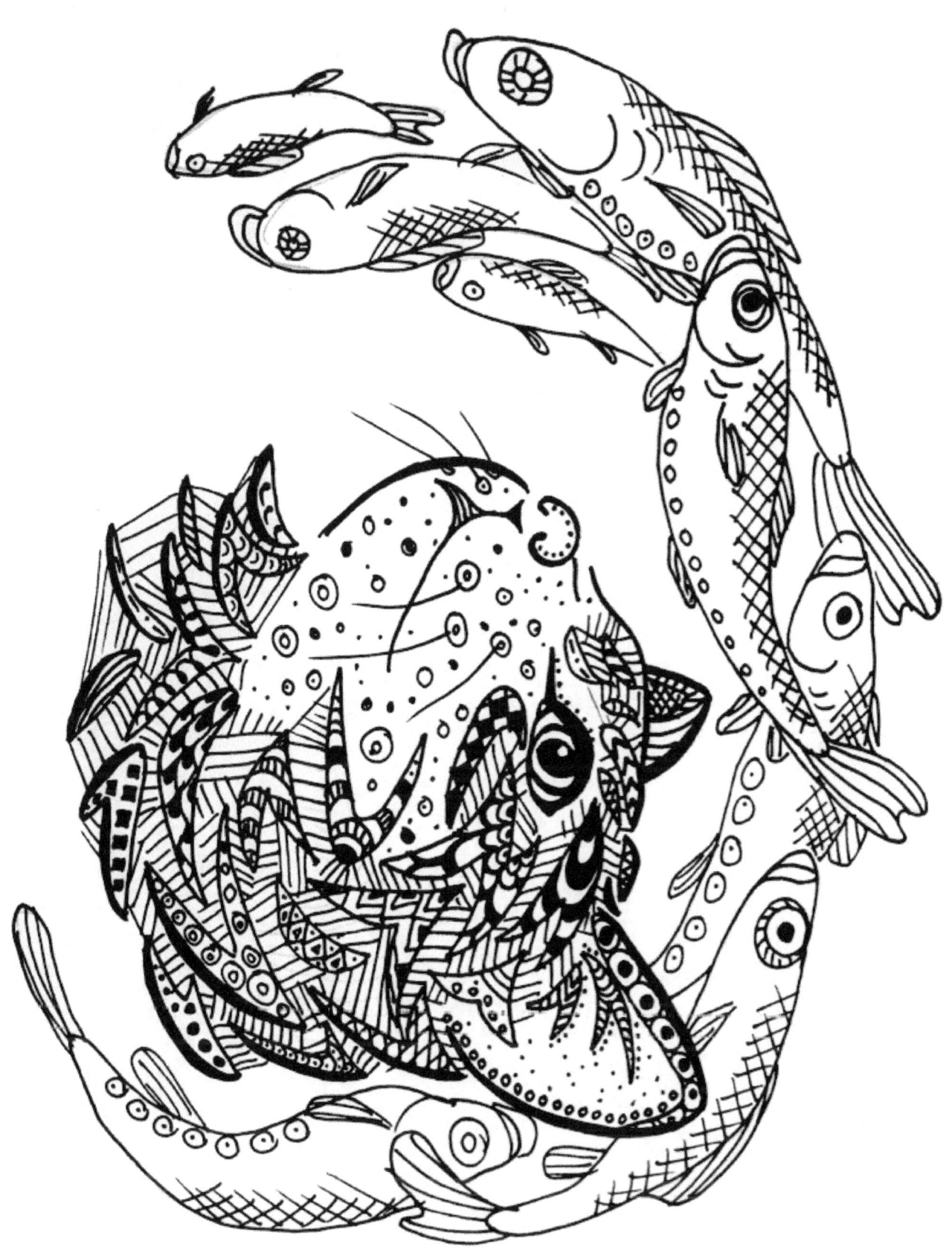

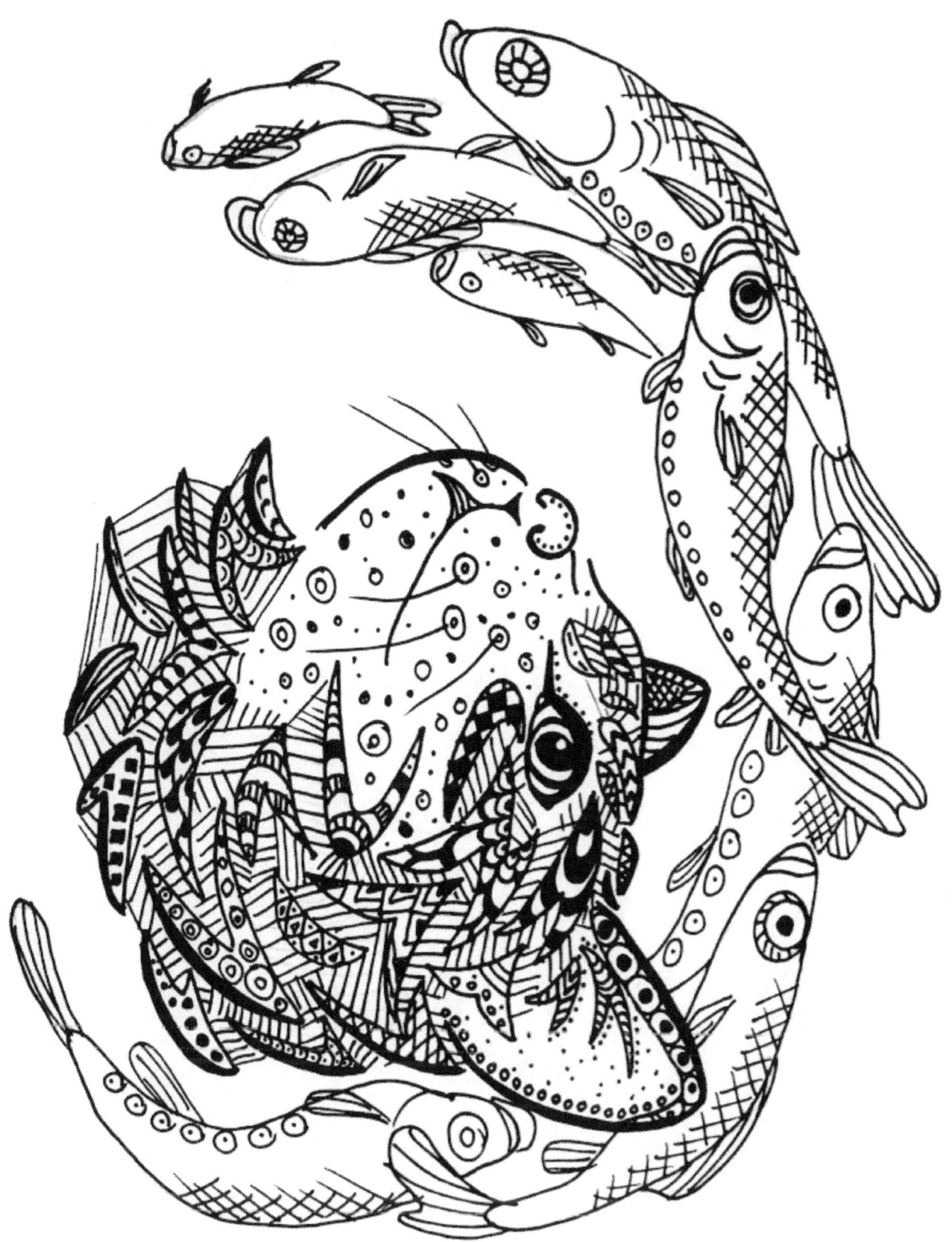

Queen Cat

I named this Zen cat a Queen Cat as she has a really royal posture. In fact, she's all kind of royalty.

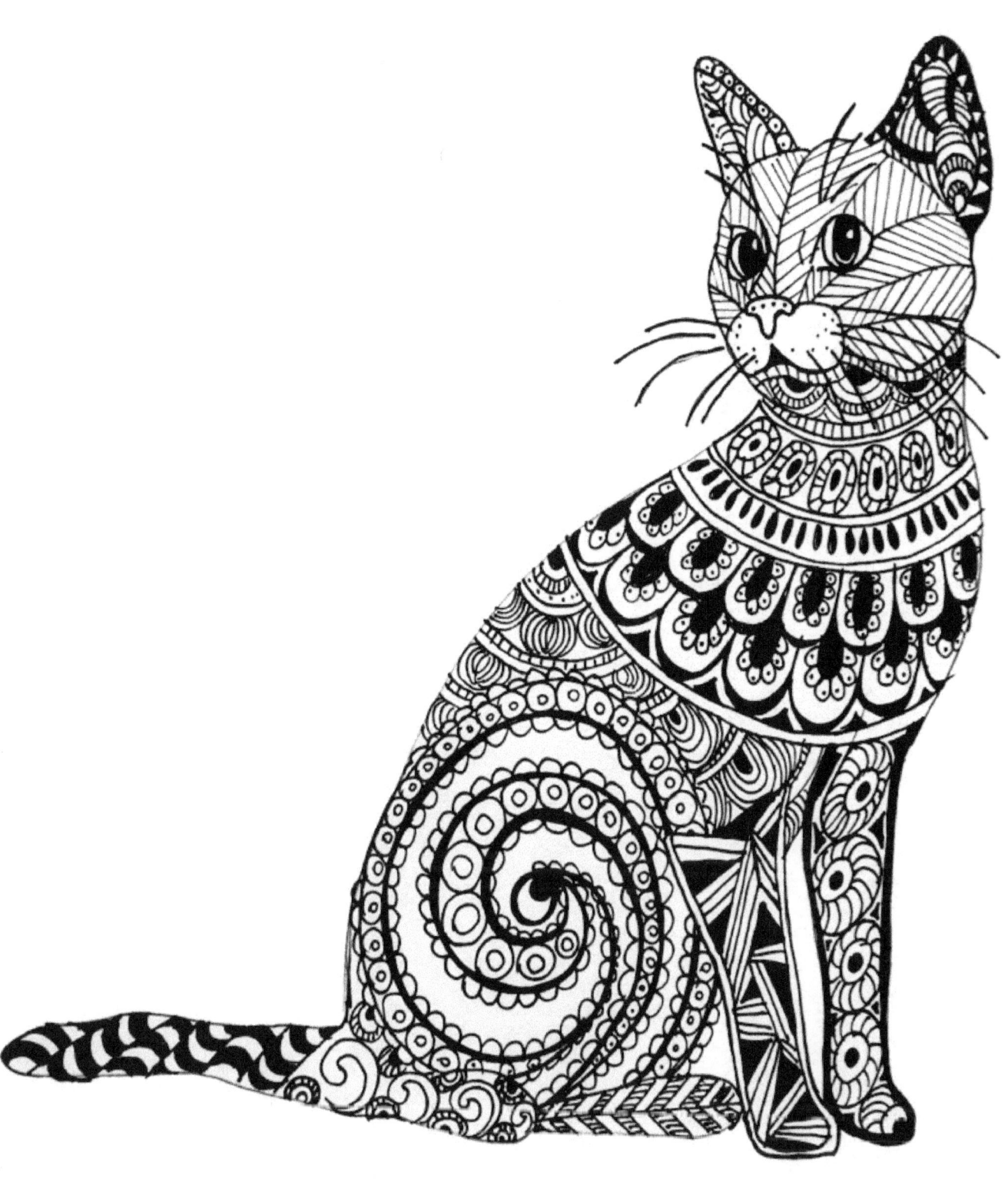

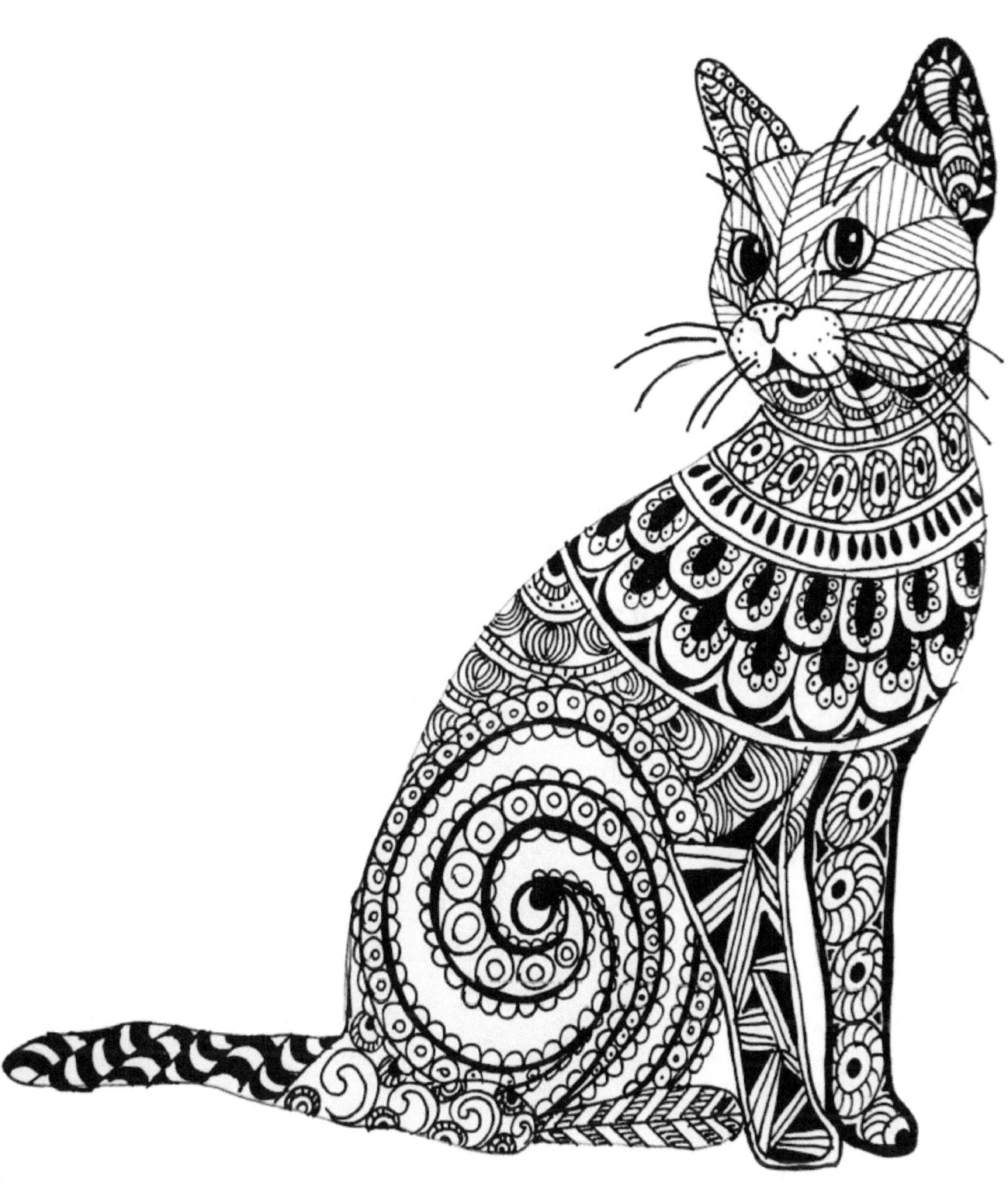

Zen Maltese

Maltese are cute and smart little dogs with white hair. People even call them "Lounge dogs" and they are ideal for those who have problems with dog hairs because they do not have a so-called undercoat. Although slightly built, they are not toys for children still they nicely match with kids and like to walk around and chase balls. Let's draw a cute little Maltese!

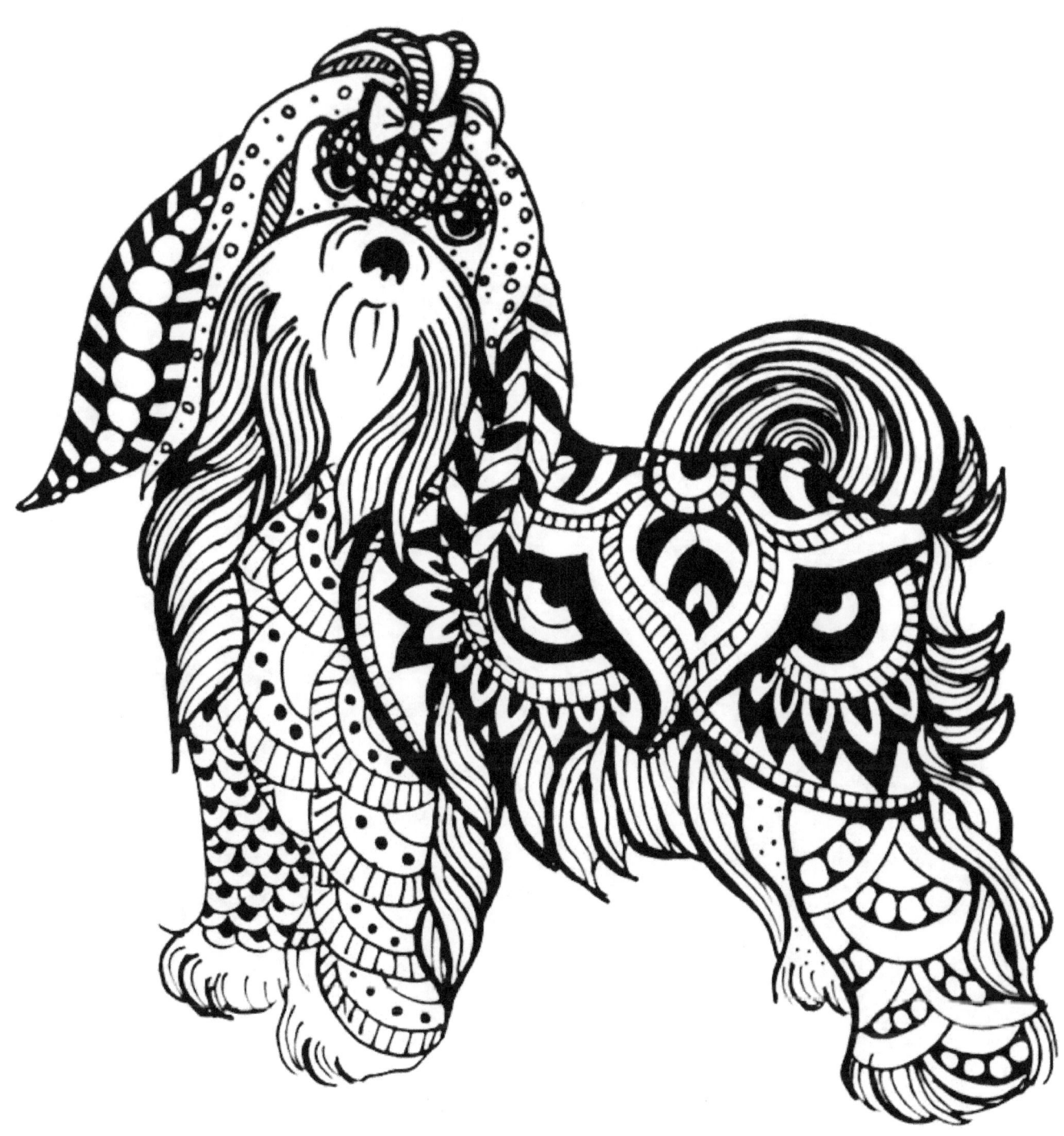

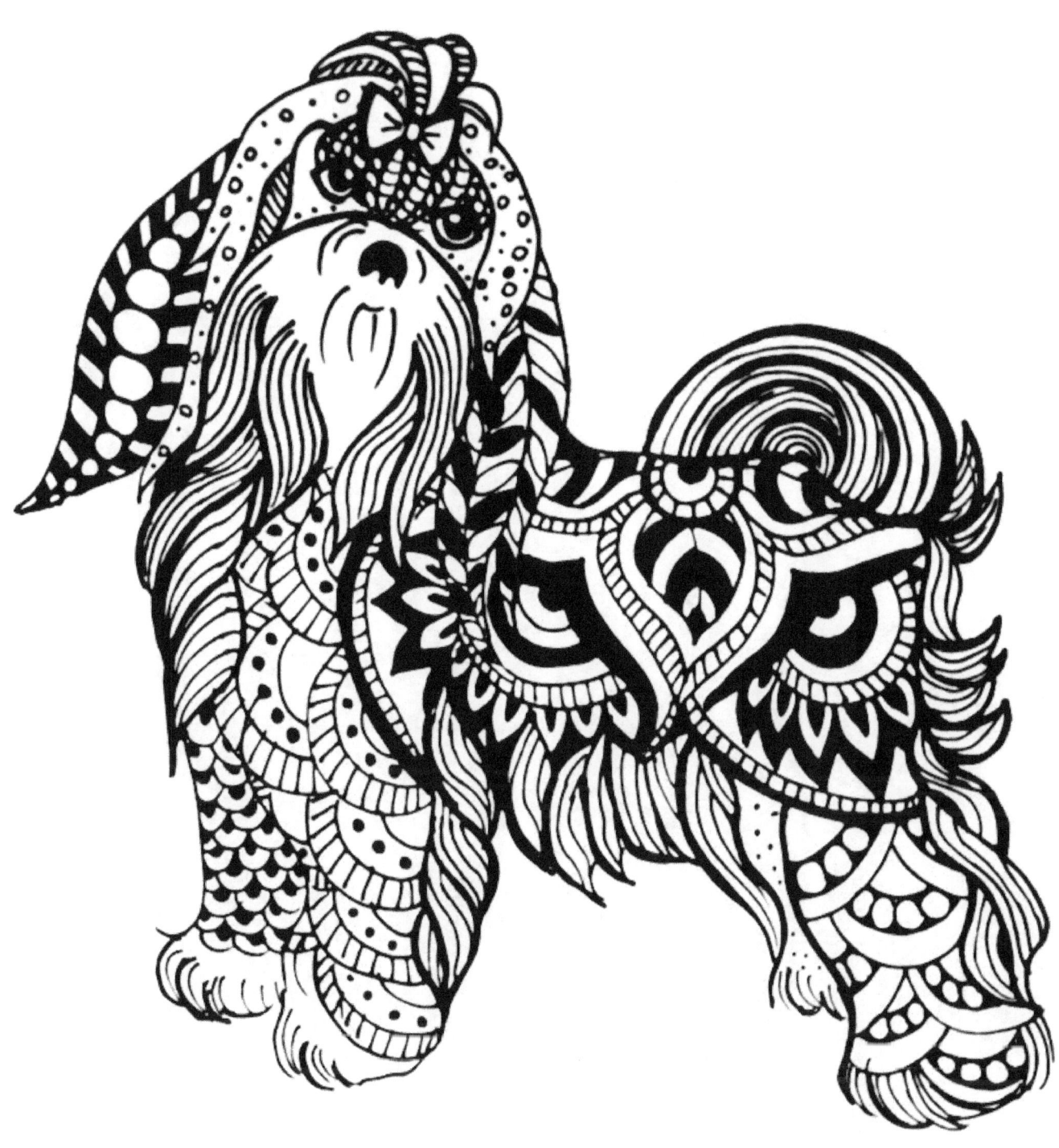

Zen Chihuahua

You have to admit that these little dogs are very cute although large spitfires. Chihuahuas can be considered as dogs "for the lap and cuddling" as they simply enjoy being with their owners. Their hearing is s very sharp and barking loud and shrill. They are known for scaring the burglars and alerting owners when there is a fire or other danger. The popularity of Chihuahuas has increased since the race became a star of Taco Bell commercials - "Yo Quiero Taco Bell."

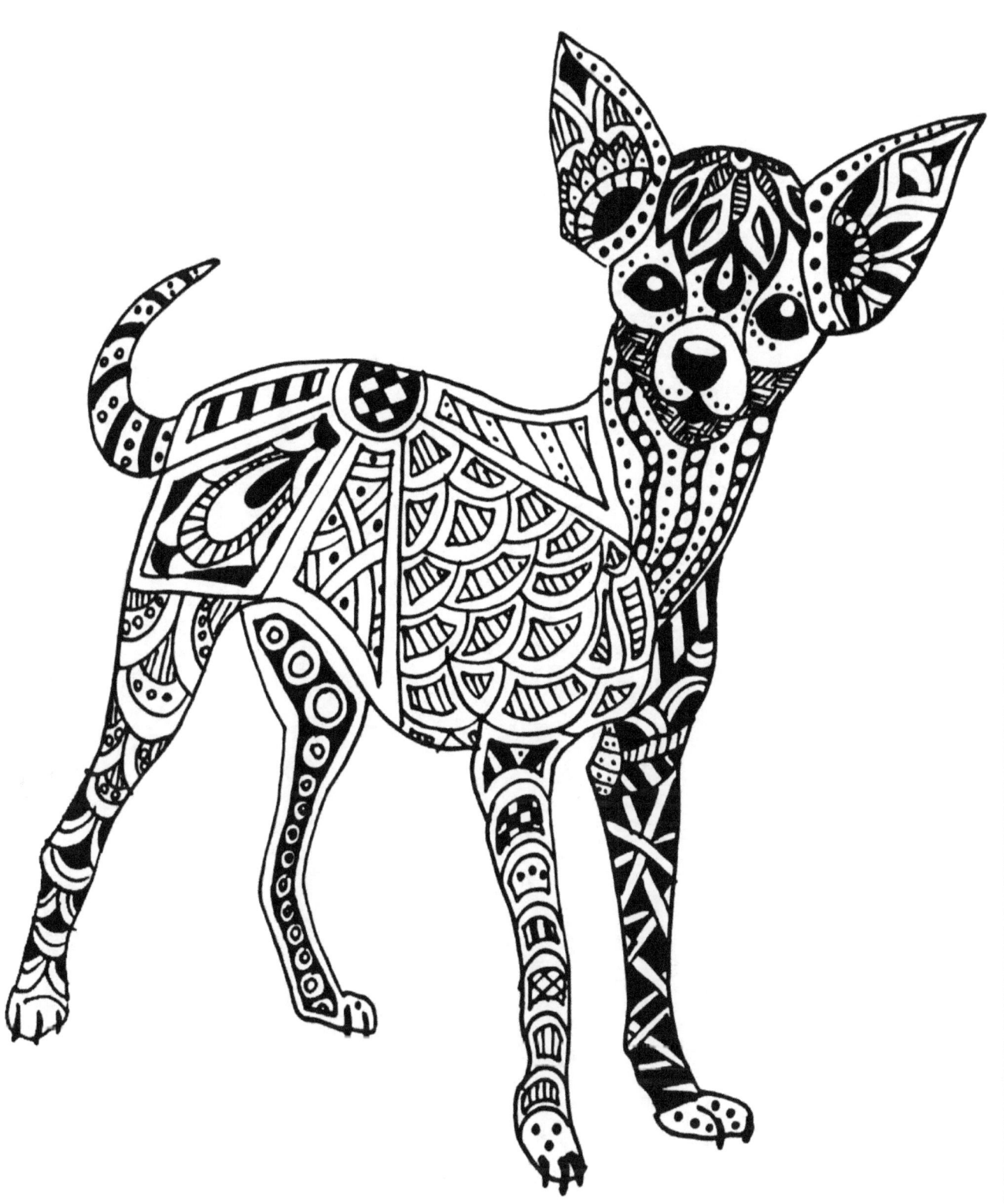

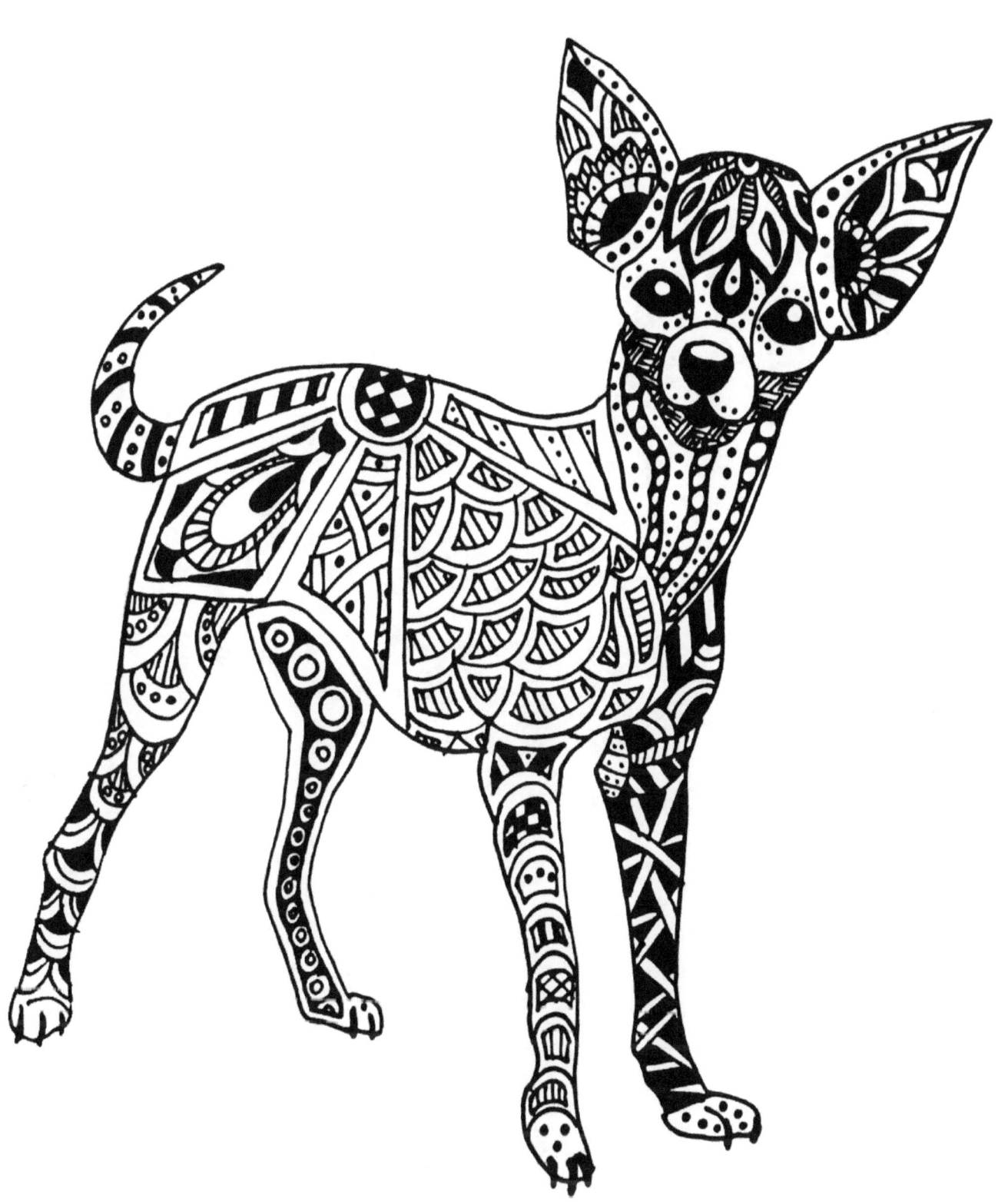

Zen Beagle: the Head

The idea was that the next Zen doodle dog represents my favorite breed, and it's a beagle. I'll always be sorry that I live in the building and cannot have this beautiful dog as a pet because he is a hunting dog and needs a lot of space to run. If you did not know, the most famous beagle in the world is Snoopy from a cartoon Charlie Brown. Now we will focus only on his beautiful head.

Beagle is otherwise very playful dog, and so it shows on the drawing, his keeps his mouth open since he is tired of running around all the time. Don`t you just love a beagle?

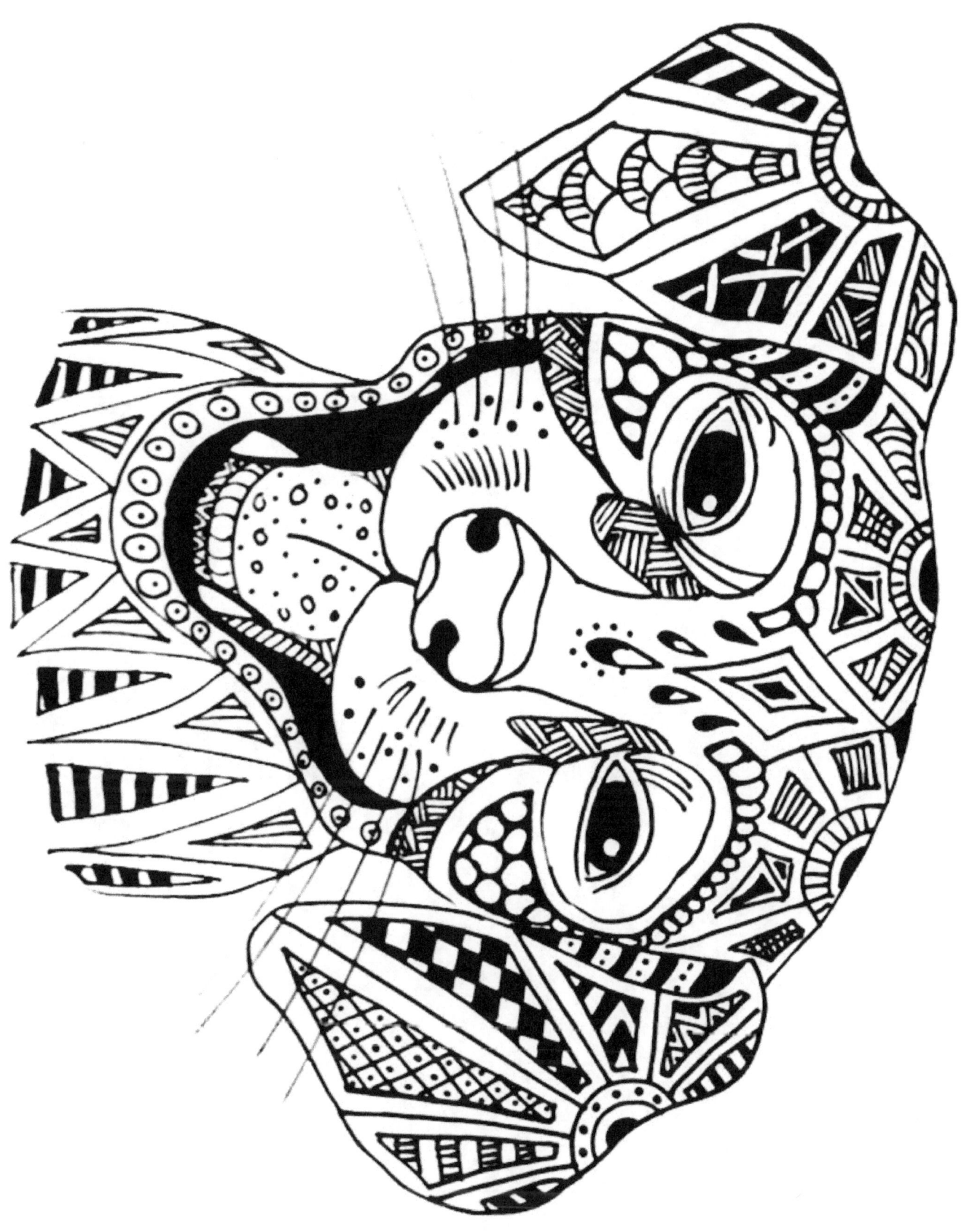

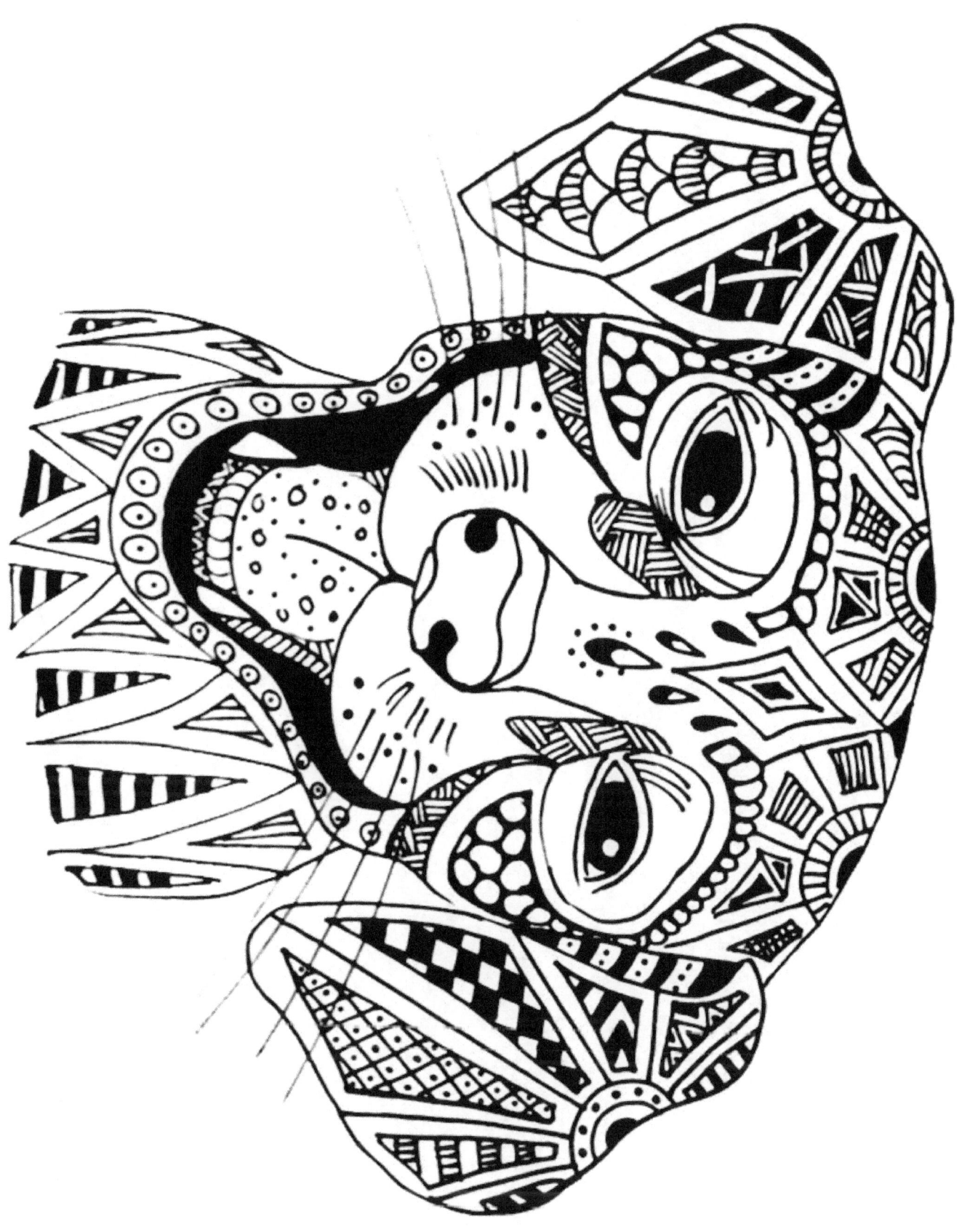

Zen Basset

Although the great hunter of rabbits, today basset is commonly kept as a pet and a show dog. This breed is basically playful, friendly, agile and active. By nature, they are very tolerant and therefore are excellent pets for families with children or other animals.

Bassets are intelligent and very easily trained with the right motivation, which in their case is food. They love to eat and will quickly understand what is required of them in order to get a treat. People wrongly believe that the Basset is stubborn which is not true. They are just very sensitive and closed if you use punishment as a training method. So, do not punish your basset hound, but give him to eat!

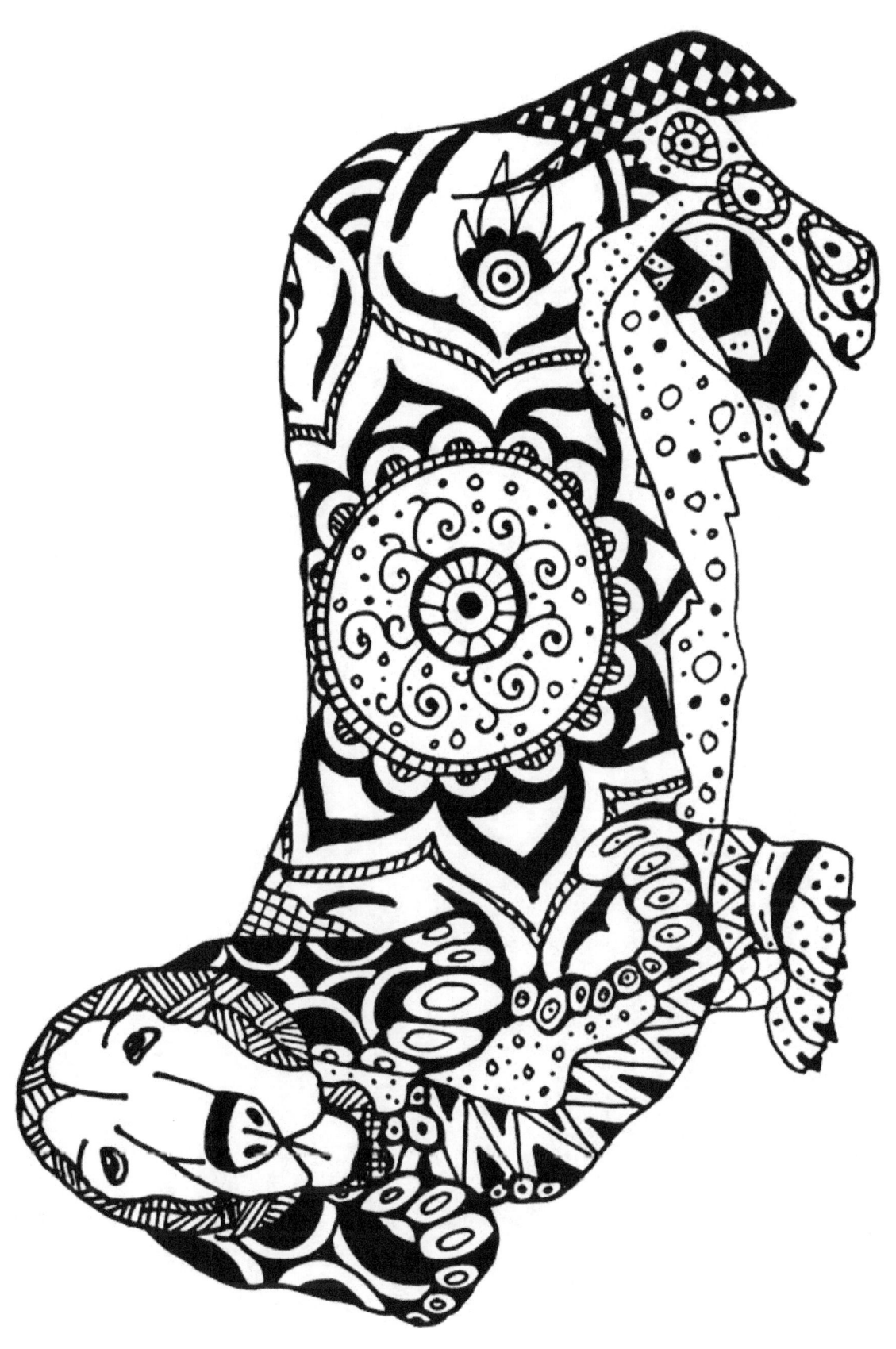

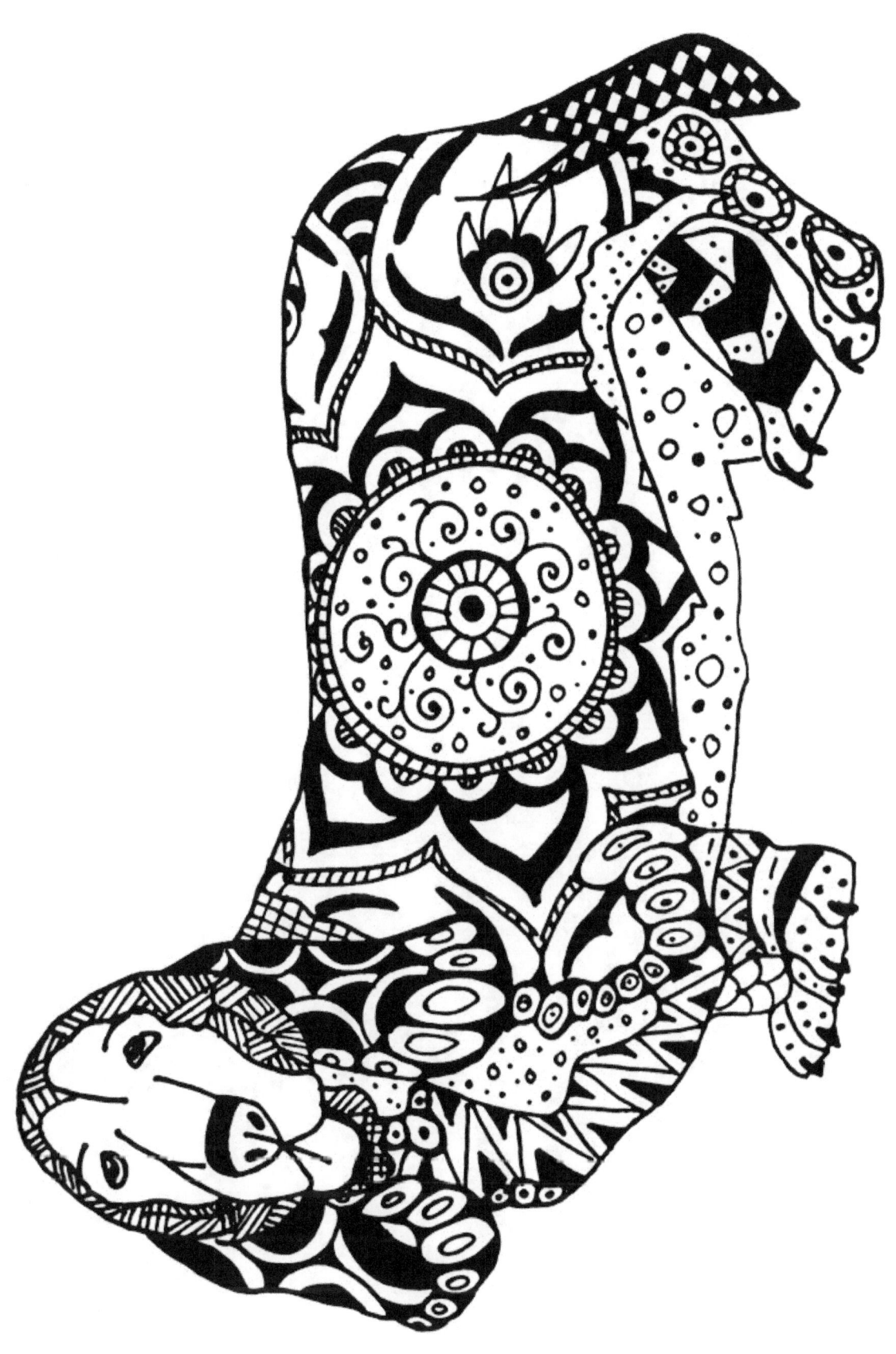

Zen Beagle: the Whole Figure

I have already introduced you with my love and affection towards the beagle, so do not be surprised that he shows up again in a book, but in a different way. The beagle that we draw before was a happy dog that looks forward to its owner. However, the beagle in this drawing is on alert and ready to hunt. In the picture below, you can see his recognizable mottle between his eyes.

The nature of the beagle is sweet and friendly both with the people and with other dogs. Beagles socialize with other dogs and the more he is with them and people, the more he is happier. This sometimes leads to problems because when left alone he constantly barks. This breed is naturally gifted in learning and is happy to learn, but there is no sense training him for a service dog as you should not expect unquestioning obedience from him. Hunting qualities of a beagle are not questionable.

If you doubt the beauty of a beagle, keep in mind that the year 2015, in March, a female beagle 'Miss P' won the 139th edition of the Westminster Kennel Club Dog Show, the most prestigious dog show in the United States held in Madison Square Garden in New York City . Miss P (What a cute name for the cute little dog!) won in competition with 2,700 dogs and almost 200 different breeds

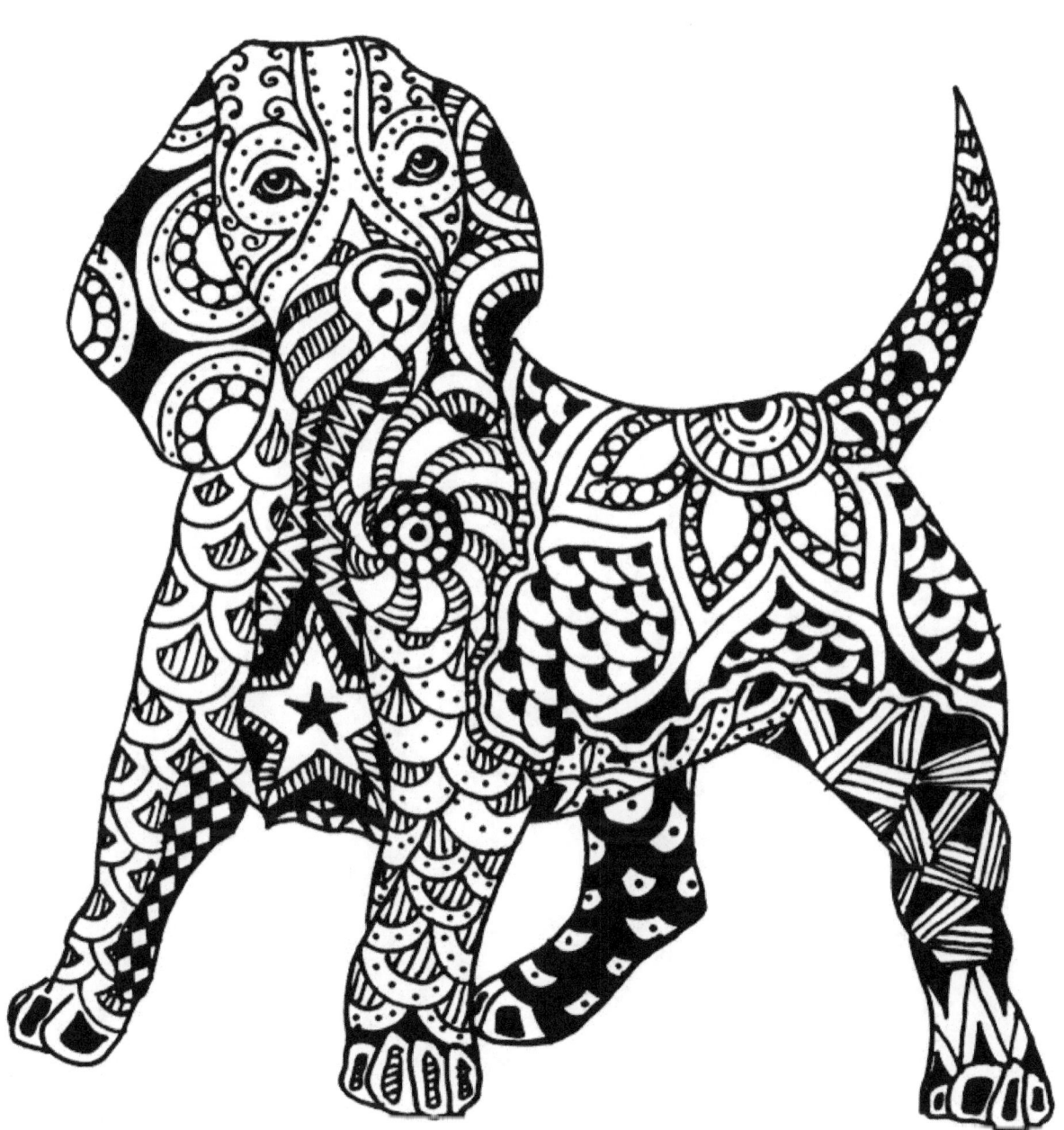

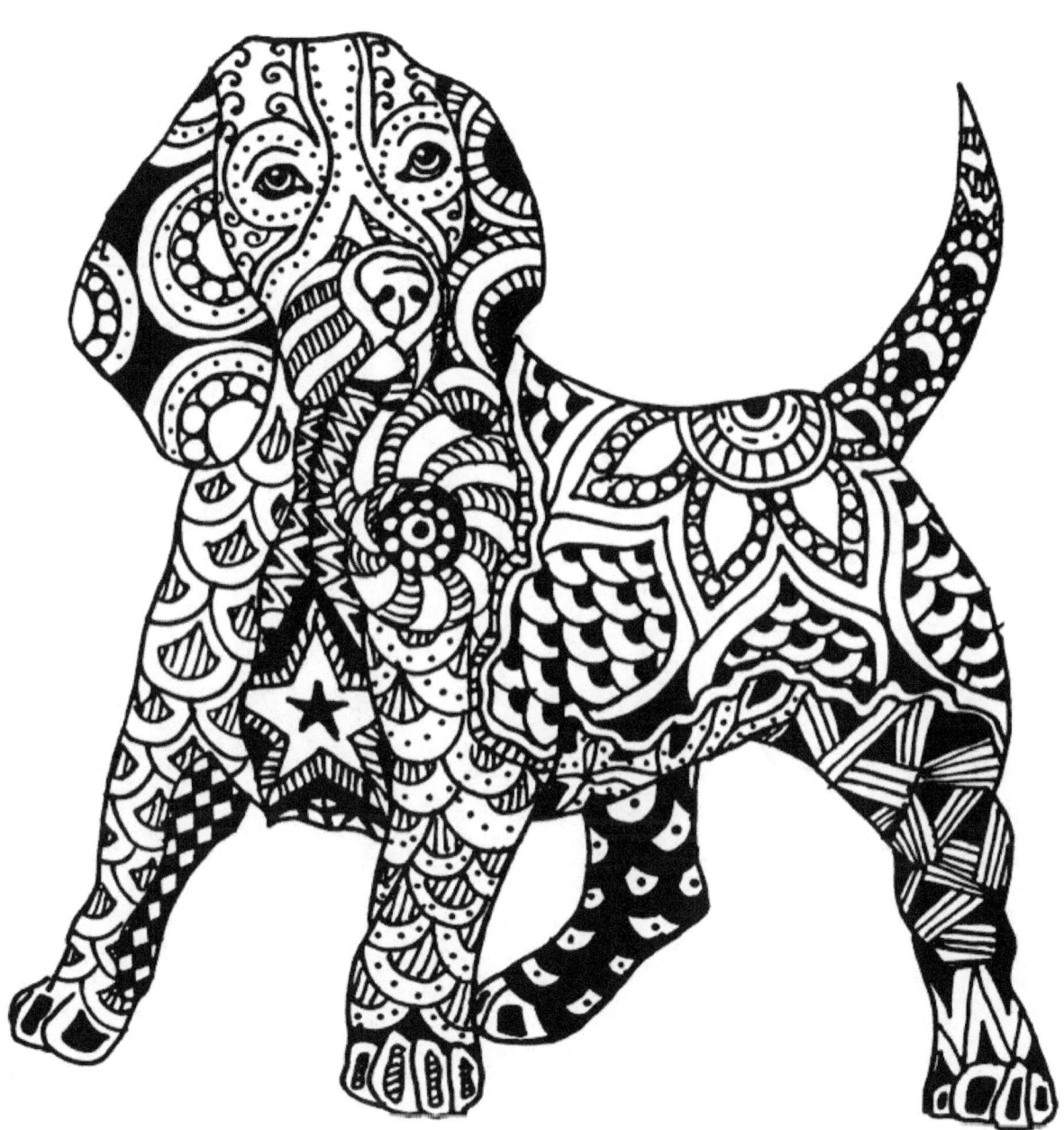

Zen Bulldog

Lovers of "dangerous" dogs would say that we have saved the best for last! Although today's bulldog descended from its aggressive ancestors, he eventually became a beautiful dog with a good nature. He is a faithful companion, a noble, strong, brave and a proud dog. Friendly look and the similar character make it the perfect pet, especially for families with children or other pets.

Bulldog generates a very strong bond with its owner, and sometimes he does not even want to go out into the yard without him. They are not very active and do not be surprised if you have to drag or carry him to the house. Their nice look and wrinkled skin attract attention; the whole park will want to pet him. So, we'll draw his very distinctive head. Pay attention to creases in the drawing below.

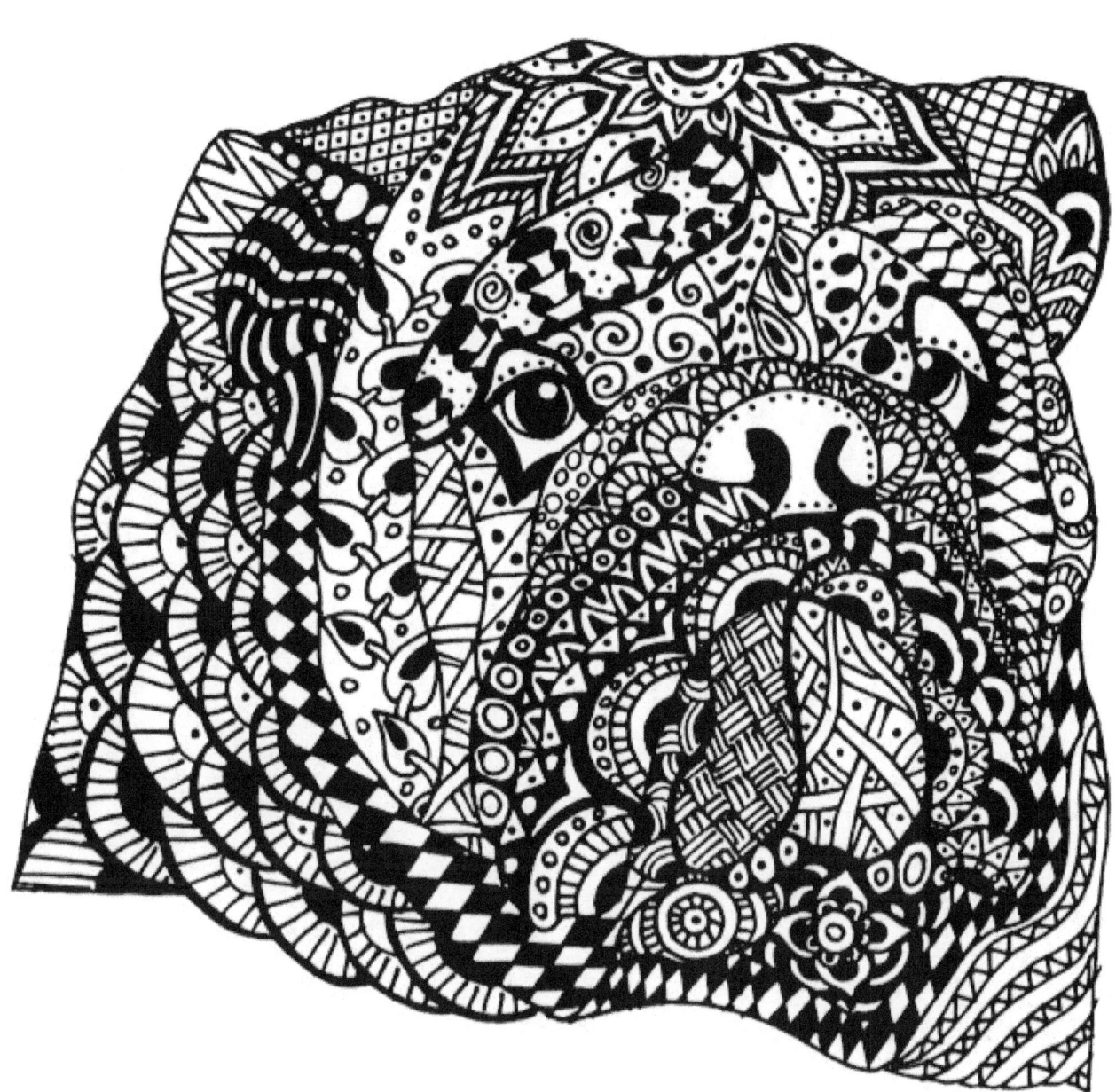

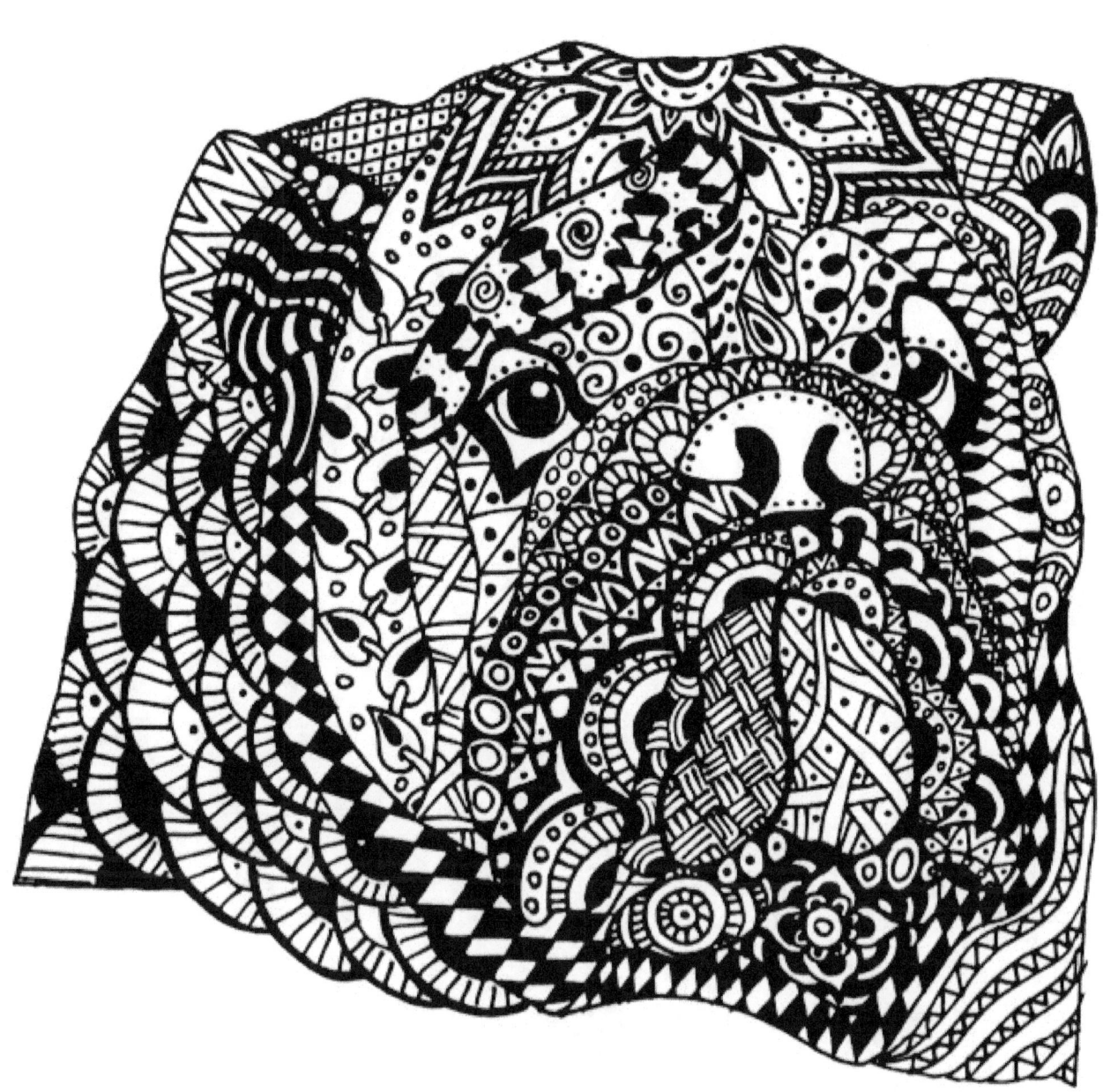

Conclusion

I really hope you enjoyed coloring my Zen Doodle Cats and Dogs! It would be really interesting for me how you colored them! But I just can imagine it. I bet everybody of you has your own particular style! Hope you had fun!

If you liked the book I would appreciate for your review. It will help me a lot!

I want to encourage you to write your review for my book – please send me the screen-short of your review to the e-mail: **kelly.artbooks@gmail.com** and you will get some **BONUS** from me as a **GIFT**!**

Thank you in advance and looking forward to see you in my other Zen Doodle coloring books!

** **in the e-mail subject please mention the name of the book you reviewed and the author.**

Thank you!

If you are interested how to draw Zen patterns form the beginning, we would be happy to recommend you other books from this author.

ZEN DOODLE: The Art of Zen Doodle. Drawing Guide with Step by Step Instructions. Book one. (Zen Doodle Art 1)

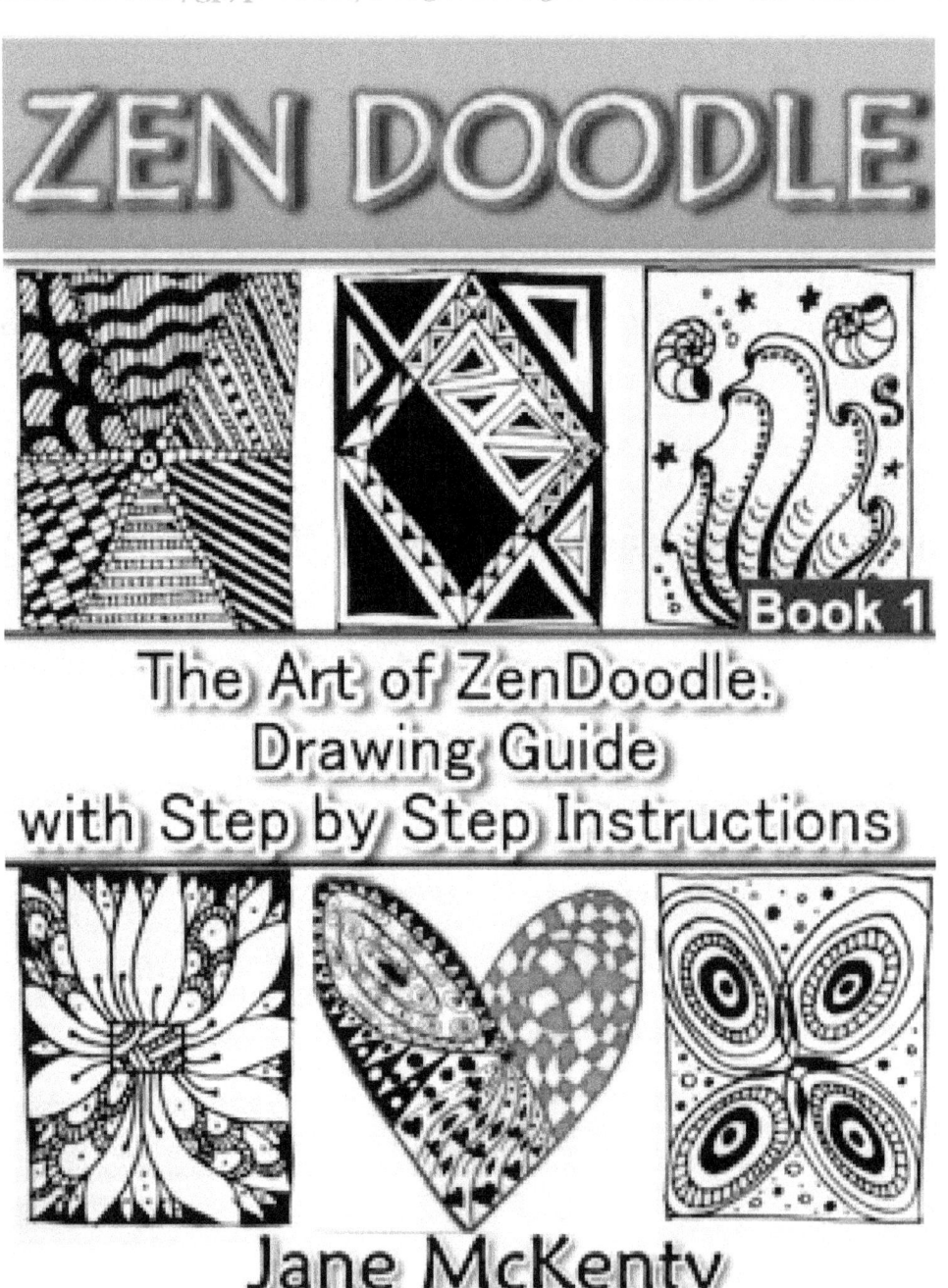

ZEN Doodle: The Art of Zen Drawing.
Master Zen Doodle with Step by Step Instructions. Book Two. (Zen Doodle Art 2)

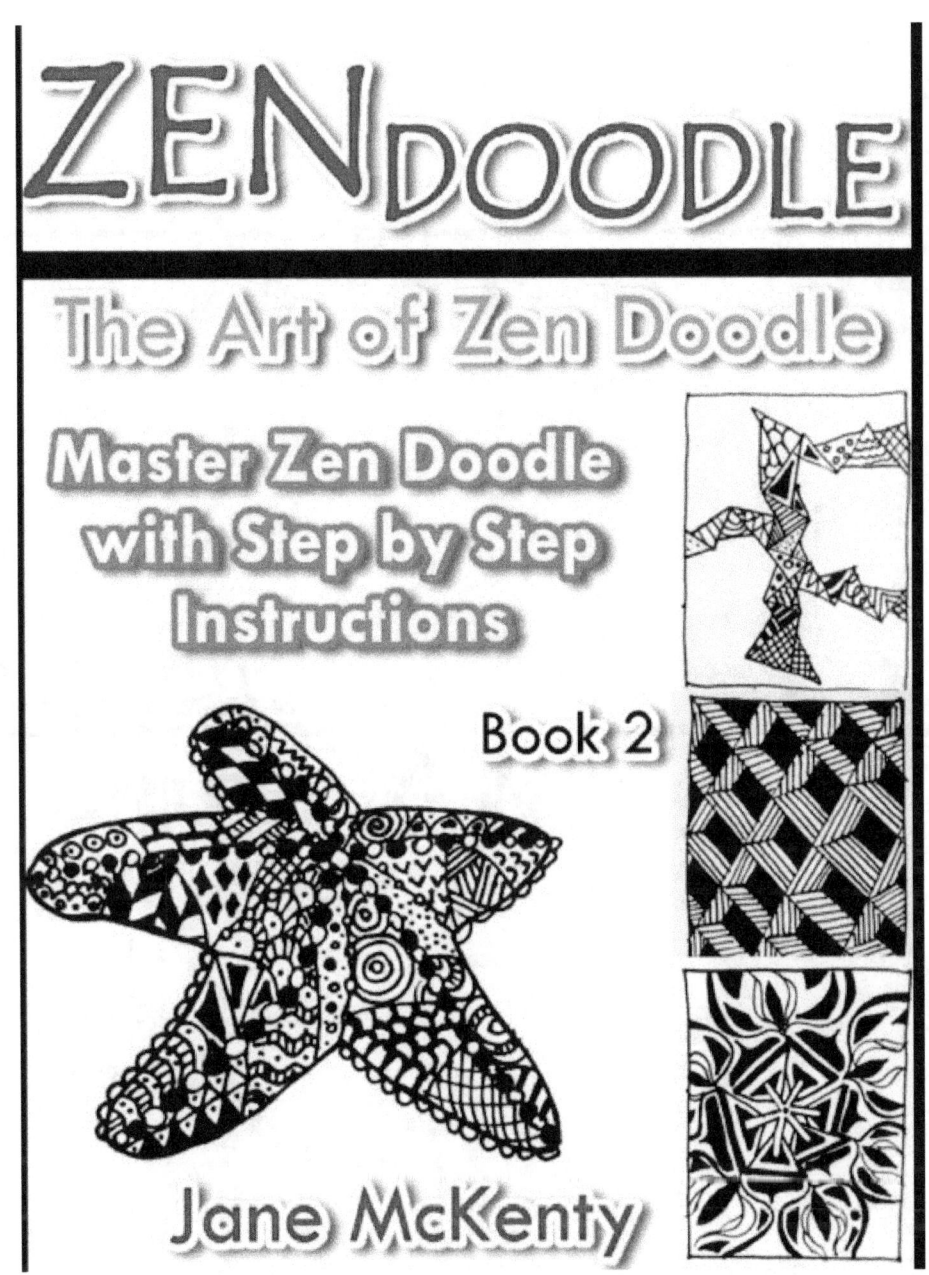

ZEN Girls: Drawing Amazing Zen Doodle Girls
(Zen Doodle Art Book 4)

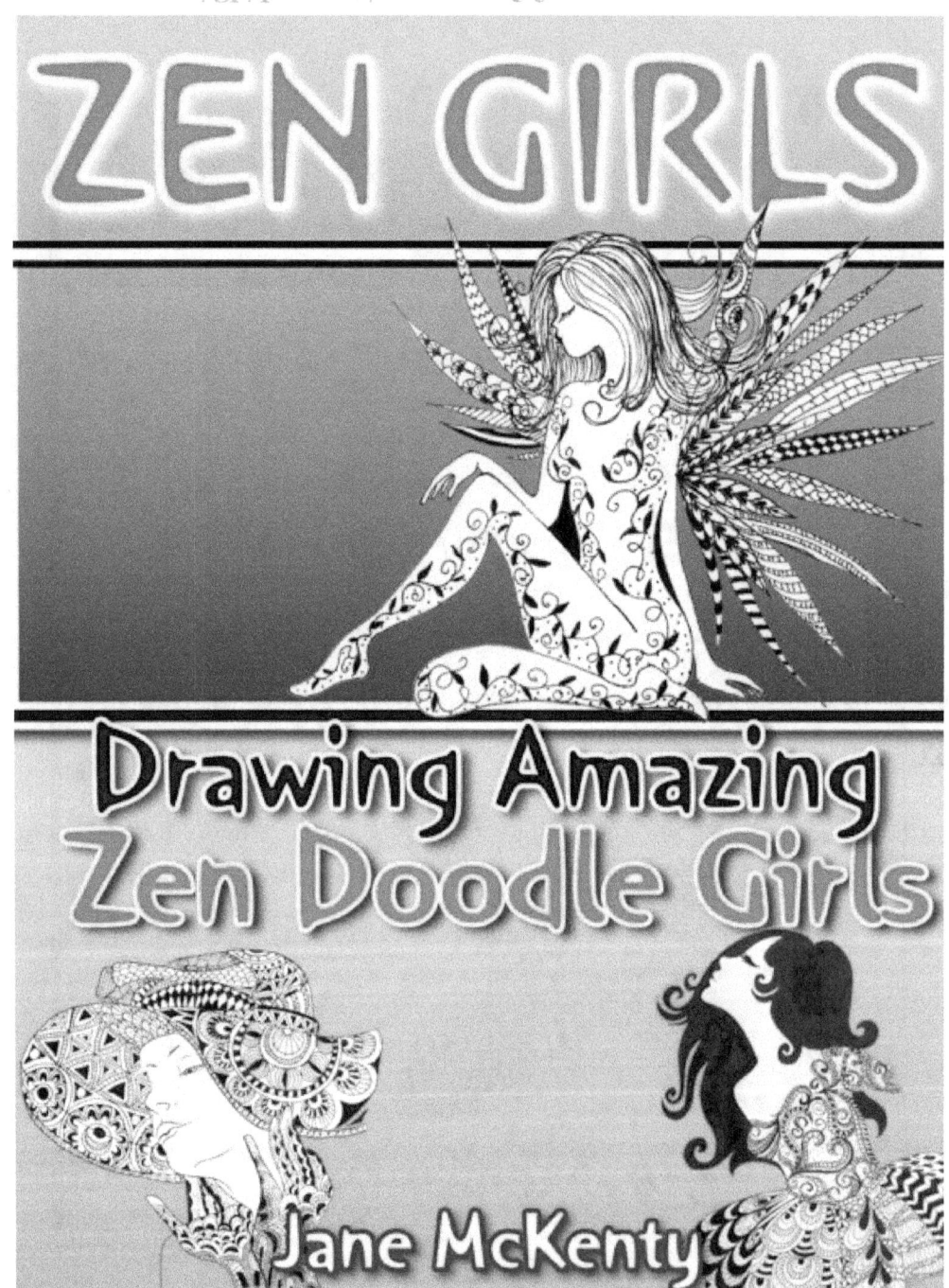

ZEN Horses: Drawing Amazing Zen Doodle Horses!
(Zen Doodle Art Book 5)

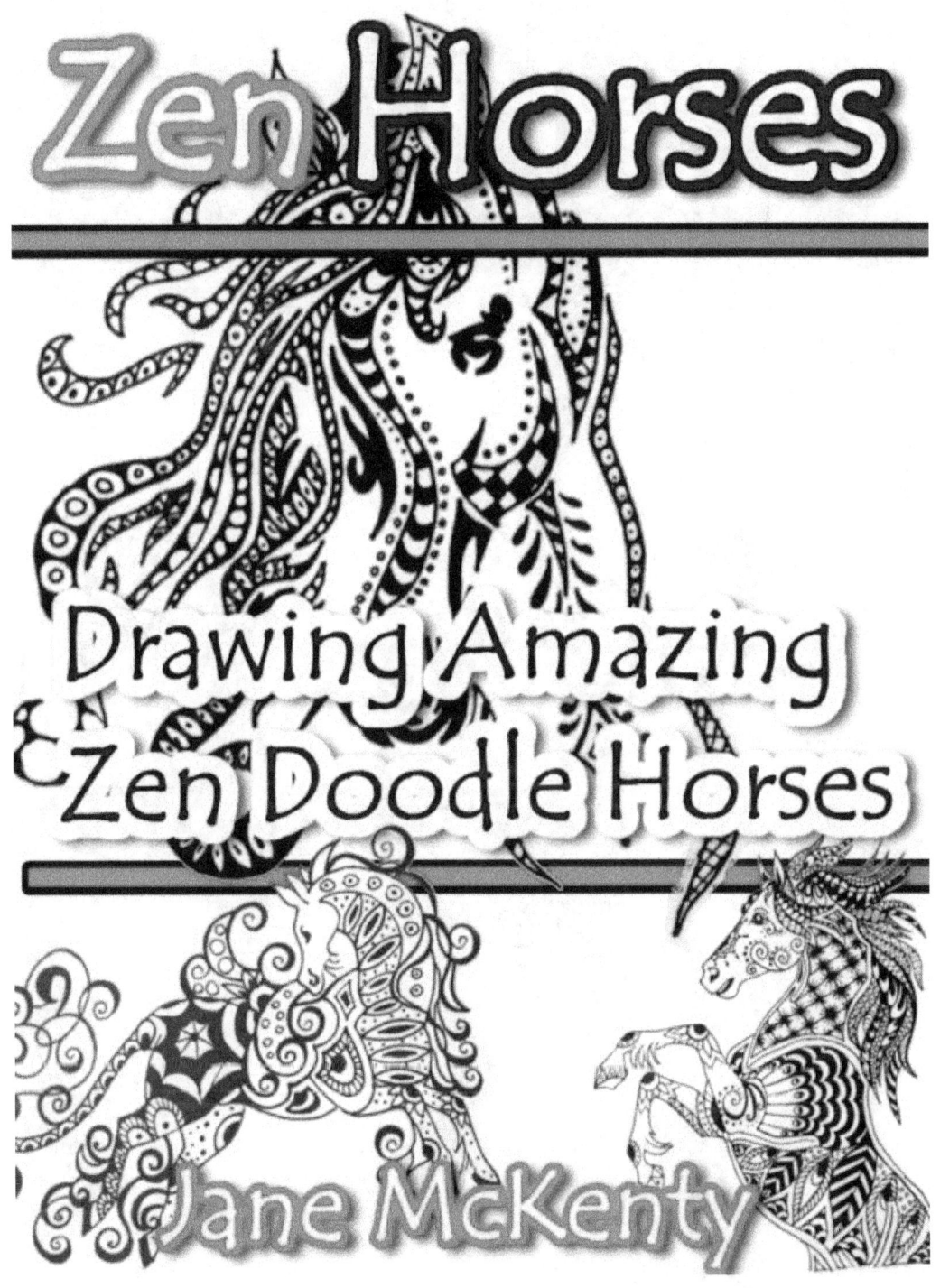

ZEN DOGS: Drawing Zen Doodle Dogs
(Zen Doodle Art Book 6)

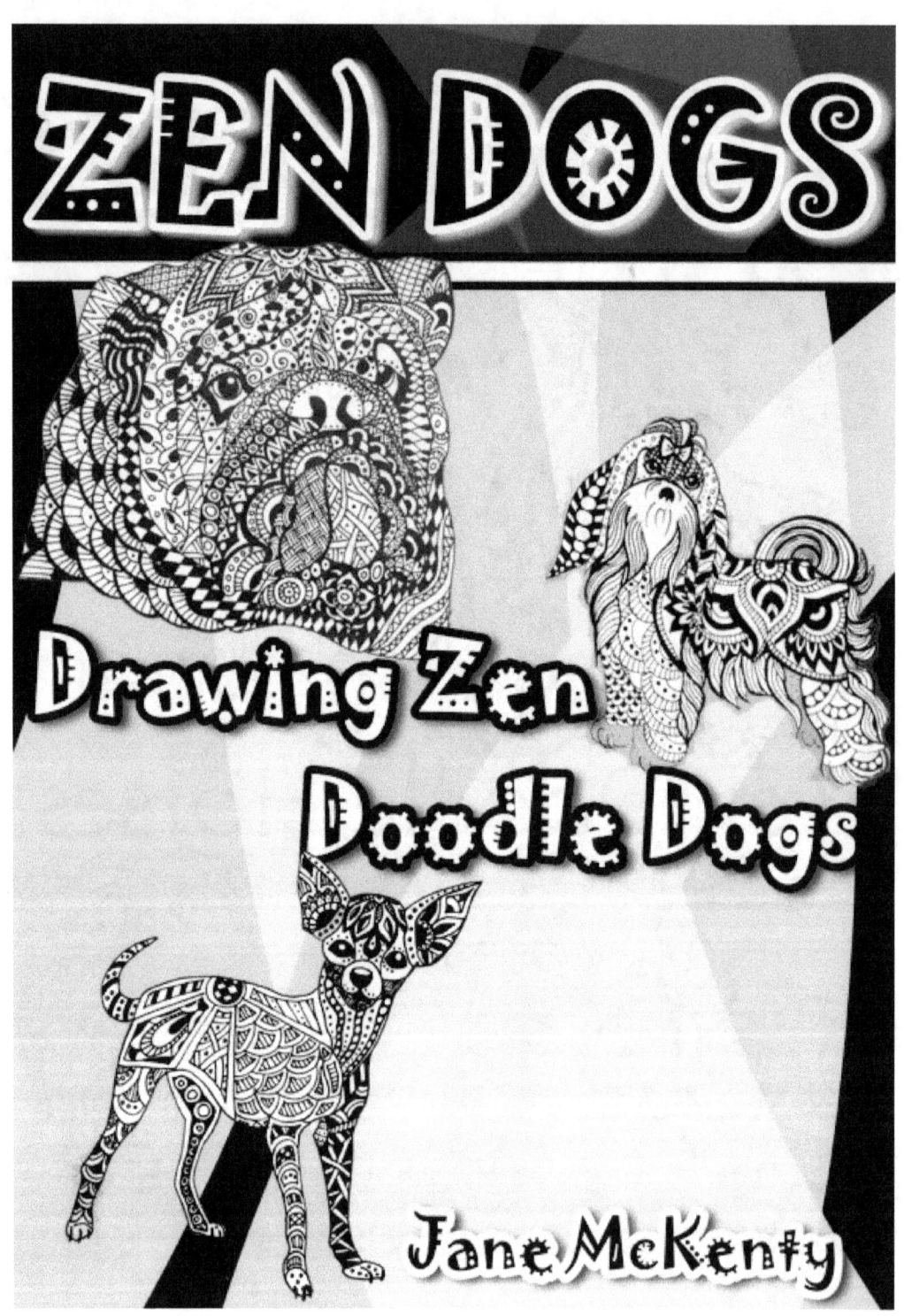

ZEN CATS: Drawing Amazing Zen Doodle Cats
(Zen Doodle Art Book 3)

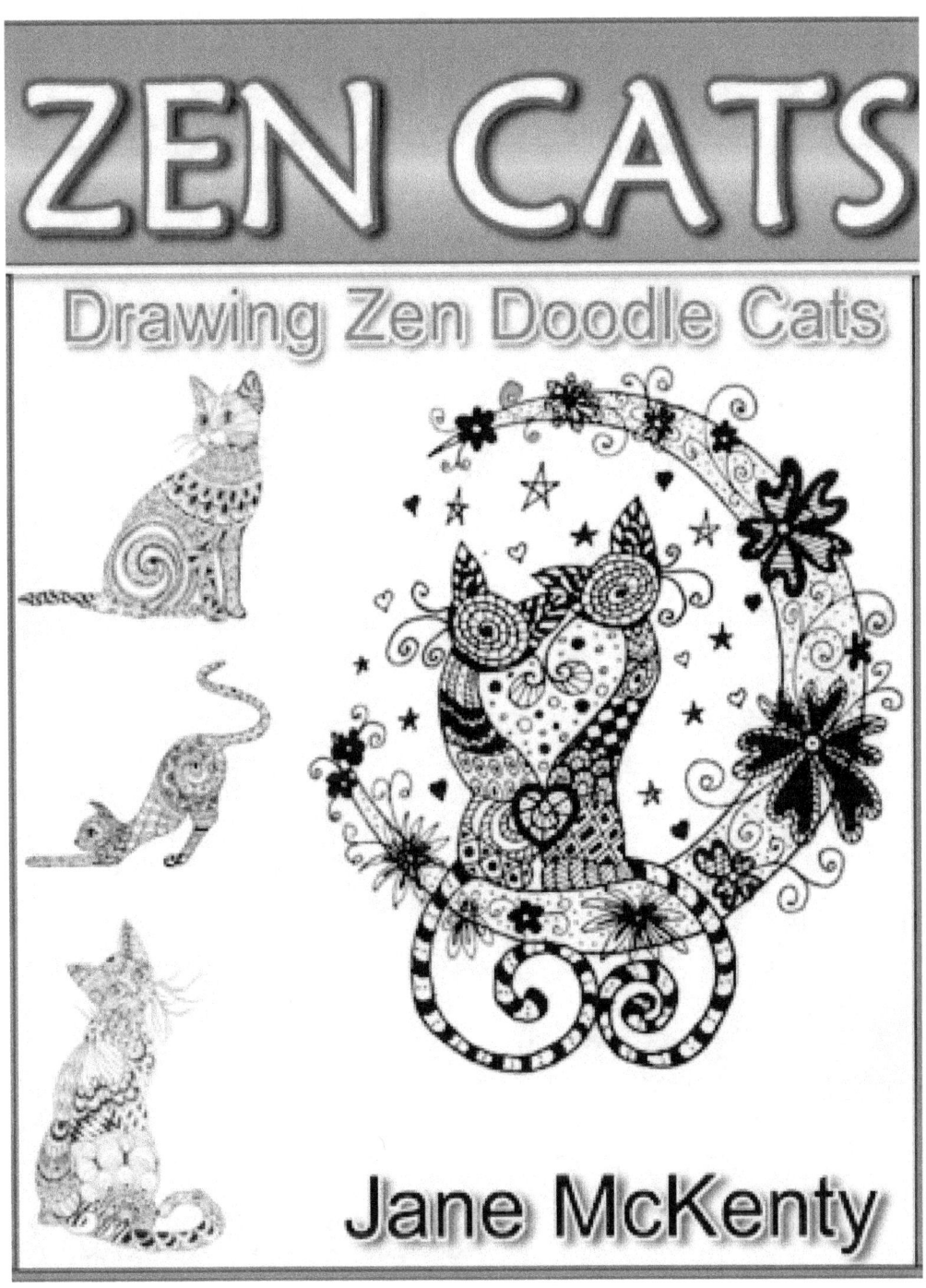

ZEN Doodle Art:

Drawing Underwater Life with Amazing Zen Doodle Technique

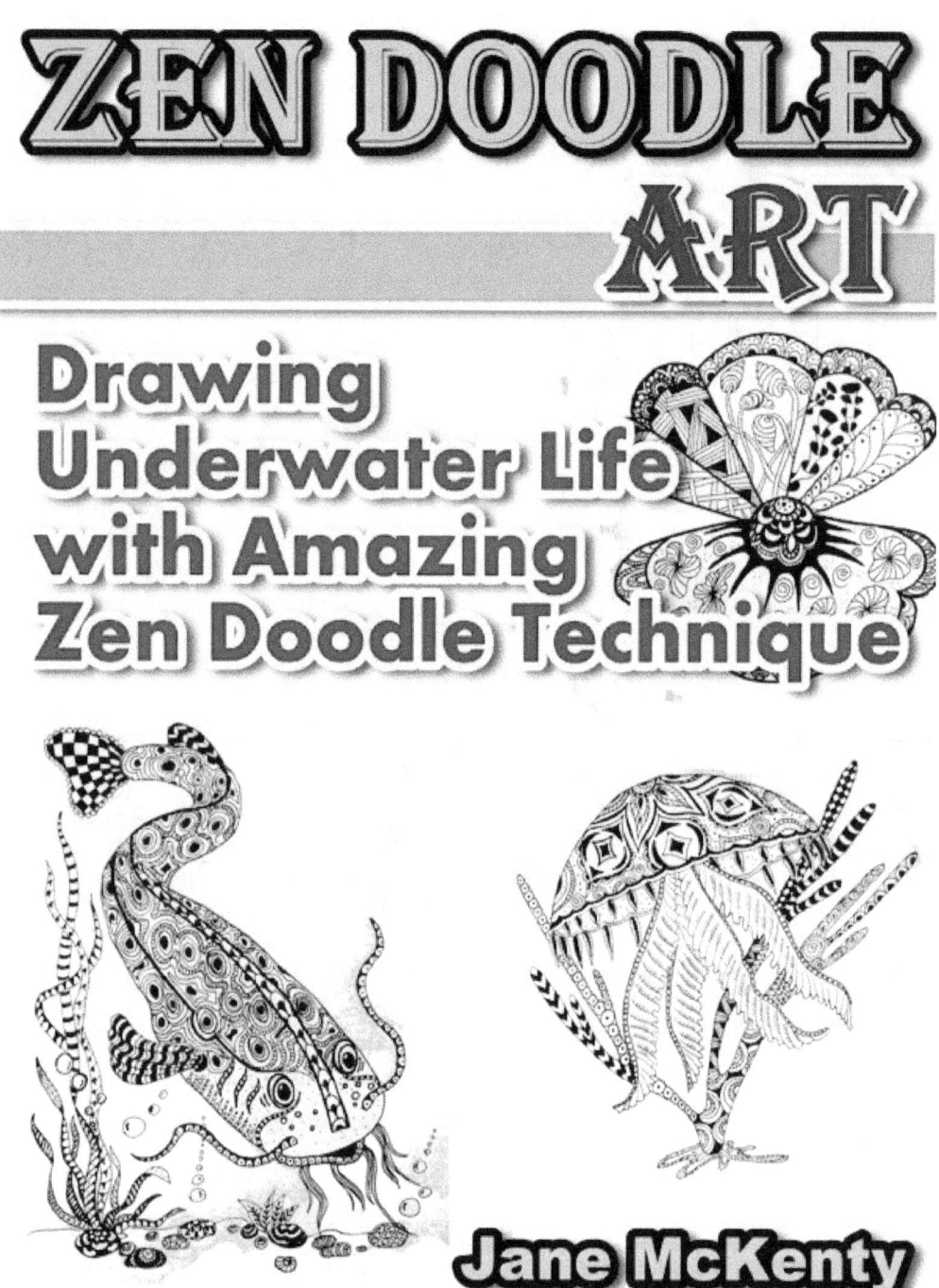

Disclaimer

While all attempts have been made to verify the information provided in this book, the author does assume any responsibility for errors, omissions, or contrary interpretations of the subject matter contained within. The information provided in this book is for educational and entertainment purposes only. The reader is responsible for his or her own actions and the author does not accept any responsibilities for any liabilities or damages, real or perceived, resulting from the use of this information.

The trademarks that are used are without any consent, and the publication of the trademark is without permission or backing by the trademark owner. All trademarks and brands within this book are for clarifying purposes only and are the owned by the owners themselves, not affiliated with this document.